THE LOSS OF THE SS TREVEAL

THE LOSS OF THE
SS TREVEAL

DORSET SHIPWRECK MYSTERY

David Pushman

DOWNSWAY BOOKS

First published in Great Britain 1999 by
Downsway Books
Downsway, The Hyde, Langton Matravers,
Swanage, Dorset BH19 3HE

ISBN: 0 9517621 2 5

Typeset in Great Britain by
Amberwood Graphics, St Johns Hill, Wareham, Dorset BH20 4NA

Printed in Great Britain by
Short Run Press, Exeter, Devon

To the memory of my late mother
Daisy Kate Pushman (née Lander)
1900 - 1998

Acknowledgements

I am grateful to the many people who gave me assistance, insights and encouragement during the preparation and writing of this book.

In the Isle of Purbeck I am particularly indebted to Harry Tatchell, who shared with me his boyhood recollections and Edward Pushman, my father, who trawled through a wealth of memories; also to John ('Kiwi') Mays for his knowledge of the Kimmeridge Ledges and Nick Ford who took me over them in his boat.

At St Ives, Brian Stevens, curator of the town's museum, and his wife, Margaret, were my guides through the fascinating Hain Collection; Mrs Elizabeth Beach, great niece of Captain Paynter, generously gave of her time and knowledge; Captain John Kemp, MBE, (now sadly deceased), whose long and distinguished career began as an apprentice with the Hain company, provided me with invaluable information and insights during many pleasant hours of conversation; the Rev Ian M Densham of the Zion Congregational Church, the Rev Steven J Wild of the Bedford Road chapel, and Mr David Allan, organist at the latter place of worship , all gave valuable assistance.

At Swansea, Malcolm Donald, son of the *Treveal*'s third officer, kindly welcomed me into his home and talked candidly about his father and the family's history.

I also wish to thank the many correspondents who wrote to me with information and the several people who allowed me an interview over the telephone: Mrs Caroline Brassington, niece of Captain Paynter, who spoke to me about her childhood memories; Mr Philip Thomas of Saltash who sent me a treasury of information about Peter Cogar, ship's carpenter; Mr Frank Argall, of Truro, who wrote with information about Frederick Argall, *Treveal* apprentice, and Mr Charles Argall, of Pinner, Frederick's brother, who kindly spoke to me on the telephone; Mrs Quick of St Ives and Mr Davies of Truro, who wrote to me about James Bassett, sailor; and Mrs Lily Stevens of St Ives and Mr Horace Noall of Calverton, who wrote to me about Tom Noall, sailor.

I must also express my thanks to the following: K Anthony Ellis of the Coastguard Museum at Bridlington and Mary Cunningham of the Marine Information Centre, Southampton, for providing much useful information; Trisha Carver at the *St Ives Times & Echo*, for making that newspaper's coverage of the *Treveal* disaster available to me and for considerable assistance besides; Josephine Jefford of the Cornish Family History Society for her help with research; also, the staffs of the Public

Record Office, National Maritime Museum and National Newspaper Library in London, the Cornish Local Studies Library, Redruth, and the Dorchester, Plymouth, Southampton, and Swansea reference libraries.

Finally, I would like to record my debt to Georgina Cook for her typing, and Mary Costello, Mike Robbins, Sue Kendall and Mike Bizley for their critical reading of the manuscript.

Picture Acknowledgements

For permission to reproduce illustrations, I gratefully acknowledge the following: Julian Cook for the cover painting of the *Treveal;* Sue Kendall and Mary Costello for the map of the Dorset coastline (p 9); Toby Snazell for the photographs of Chapman's Pool (p10), Portland Harbour (p65), the *Treveal* cabin door (p140) which was photographed with the permission of the owners Leslie Turner (now deceased) and his son Gerald of Swanage; and the *Treveal* table (p146) which was photographed with the permission of the owner, Mr E G Wright of Swanage; St Ives Museum for the photographs of Treloyhan Manor (p23) and the *Treveal* (p33); Graham Chester for the photographs of the Hain door (p26), and Peter Cogar's headstone (p175); Elizabeth Beach for the photograph of Charles Paynter (p37); Malcolm Donald for the photograph of William Donald (p45); Frank Argall for the photograph of Frederick Argall (p62) which was taken by E C Argall of Truro; Arthur Grant/ *Daily Echo* for the photographs of the *Treveal* (p128 and p138); Philip Thomas for the letter written by Horace Piercey (p136); and Brian Bleese for the photograph of the *Treveal* cross (p176) which was made available to be photographed by Major J C Mansel of Kimmeridge. The photographs of Frank Lander (p79), the *Treveal* (p106) and the volunteer life-saving company (p122) are from the author's own collection. The publishers have been unable to trace the copyright holders of the photograph of Horace Piercey (p73), which is taken from the *Swanage Times*, and the photograph of Edward Hain (p19) which is taken from *Hain of St Ives* by K J O'Donoghue and H S Appleyard - and would be pleased to hear from the parties concerned.

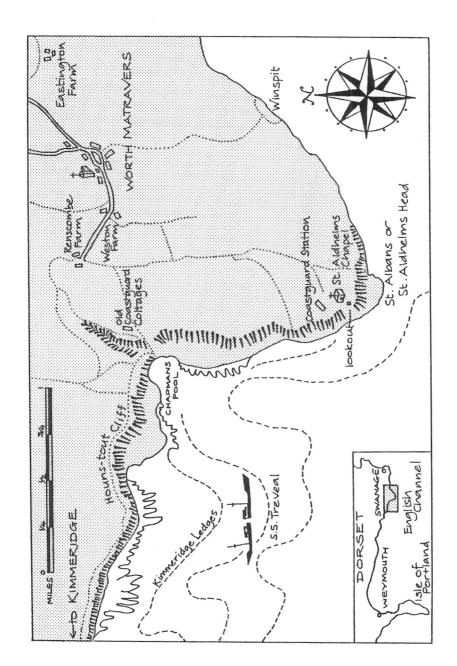

WORTH MATRAVERS

Eastington Farm

Winspit

Renscombe Farm

Weston Farm

old Coastguard Cottages

Coastguard Station

St. Aldhelms Chapel

St. Albans or St. Aldhelms Head

lookout

Houns-tout Cliff

CHAPMANS POOL

← to KIMMERIDGE

MILES

Kimmeridge Ledges

S.S. Treveal

DORSET

WEYMOUTH

SWANAGE

English Channel

Isle of Portland

The Dock

CHAPMAN'S POOL

Egmont Rocks

The Lake

Introduction

The loss of the SS *Treveal* off the Purbeck coast of Dorset in 1920 is one of the most extraordinary and melancholy stories in the annals of shipwreck. Not since the *Halsewell* was wrecked in 1786, a tragedy described by Charles Dickens in *The Long Voyage,* had a shipwreck on that notorious stretch of coast resulted in such a heavy loss of life.

The *Treveal,* a cargo steamer, owned by the Hain Steamship Company of St Ives, was returning from Calcutta to Dundee on her maiden voyage. On the evening of Friday 9 January, in mysterious circumstances, she went aground on the Kimmeridge Ledge, half a mile from the nearest shore. During the night the weather deteriorated and the following morning, at nine o'clock, the captain, fearing the vessel was about to break up, decided to abandon ship. The crew got away in two boats and rowed for the shore. At Chapman's Pool, just 50 yards from the beach, the boats capsized, and 36 men out of 43 were drowned in the churning surf.

Four months after the disaster, a formal inquiry was held at Weymouth. Two judges, assisted by three naval assessors, listened for seven days to the evidence of witnesses and the speeches of counsel for the various parties. In closing the inquiry the president of the court said: 'I should like ... to thank all those concerned who have come forward to help the Court through all these long days of sitting, and to express, what everyone feels, our great grief at what happened on that fateful day, 9 January. The secret of how that ship came on the Ledge is lost in Chapman's Pool ... It was an awful day and an awful fatality, and it is shrouded in mystery.'

Growing up in the Purbeck village of Worth Matravers between the Wars the *Treveal* entered my consciousness at an early age. Through the summer months children could be found at Chapman's Pool sitting astride spars of wood, paddling them around the rocks. The 'ships' ranged from brave little tugs to great waterlogged dreadnoughts. In winter, gales took the spars far out to sea, but in the spring, much to our joy, there they would be, back again. Sometimes, someone would run a spar up on to a sloping rock and pretend to be the *Treveal.* These games were played in complete innocence, for we had been kept in ignorance of the awful details of the *Treveal* story. It was a subject rarely talked about by our elders, and I remember being tantalised by the pervasive silence surrounding what was surely one of the most significant events in the history of our village. What lay behind the silence? What part had

Worth Matravers and its people played in the disaster?

So far as I knew, my grandfather, Frank Lander, and the curate of Worth Matravers, the Reverend Horace Piercy, had been the heroes of the hour. Over the years I was to learn a great deal more. I kept my eyes and ears open. Some of the things I heard have never been spoken of outside of the village; some have never been spoken of outside of my family. By the time I was a young man I had stored away in my head scores of anecdotes relating to the *Treveal* and to the locks, catches, items of cutlery, tables and doors, which had come from the ship . Over time many of these relics have been scattered further afield - across Dorset and beyond. A clock, reputedly from the ship, gravitated to Scotland some years ago; another relic found its way into the possession of M F C Adam of Bedfont in Middlesex: 'It is a dragon carved in black oak. Mrs. Polly Andrews of Corfe Castle gave it to me some years ago ... Polly was a life-long friend of my mother ...' (*Dorset*, No 58, p 26).

As a boy, everything I saw to do with the *Treveal* filled me with wonderment, and everything I heard - all the stories and fragments of stories - I mentally stored away without discrimination. Later, the quest to learn about those people in the *Treveal* story of whom I had no direct knowledge would take me as far afield as the scattered relics of the ship herself - and I would hear many more tales. Today, I can say that the 'truth' of some of the stories is to be found only in the fact of their invention: these were stories people told themselves in order to help them cope with the trauma they had faced. Other stories I heard, though, have proved to be factually accurate, and shed light on aspects of the *Treveal* disaster, which the official inquiry failed to illuminate.

The story of the loss of the *Treveal* is the story of a dour steam tramp, her crew, and the people who inhabited the wild stretch of coast where she was wrecked. It is a story of workaday seafaring - raised out of the everyday by the extraordinary circumstances of the ship's loss.

Chapter 1

On 10 January 1995, the 75th anniversary of the *Treveal* disaster, I was sitting at a desk, pondering how to tell the story, which I had prevaricated over for the best part of a lifetime. The hours flew by and my anxiety grew in the face of a self-imposed ultimatum: if I couldn't begin the story on this day, then I never would. I walked across to the window, undid the catch and stood looking at the washed-out view. The coastal villages between Weymouth and Swanage are not on the coast as such but follow another line, a mile or two inland, where some hollow, knoll or belt of trees affords a measure of shelter from the south-west gales which lash the coast through winter. Worth Matravers is one such village. It lies in a barely perceptible south-tilted hollow. From the upper window, through which I was then gazing, I could glimpse the English Channel, a mile away to the south down Winspit combe, at that season and time of day, barely distinguishable from the vast sky; to the south-west rose the broad back of St Aldhelm's Head, now vulgarly called St Alban's, as the Dorset historian Hutchins noted long ago; and due west, but invisible from the village, lay the small, horseshoe-shaped cove called Chapman's Pool. After sweeping the distant horizon, my eyes came to focus on the foreground: the tops of the buildings in the heart of the village were visible in the late afternoon gloom, and just beyond I could not see but could visualise the cottage of my late grandfather, Frank Lander.

It was as clear to me then as it had been as a child. It was 'Down the Lane'. On a still summer's evening Winspit would 'open out', showing off its lynchets and the violet-tinted sea - the colours of the day slowly fading. Here was cottage husbandry. The sturdy cottage, the donkey shed, fat brown hens, the garden with its thick, black, loamy soil, the galvanised iron shed where the lobster pots were made, and the nearby withy bed, dotted with yellow primroses and celandines. Inside the cottage smelt of past generations, eating the same food, wearing the same clothes and warming around the same kitchen range. A grey oilcloth would be put on the table for a meal. It might be lobster, a fat-clawed crab or some deep red Chapman's Pool prawns. A brass oil lamp would flicker, to burn off its black tip, and a kettle would simmer gently over the warm range. There was a framed picture of General William Booth in the coal hole, a calendar, with a cardboard pouch to hold Old Moore's Almanac, and some floriferous china ornaments. In the window recesses were geraniums, smelling like wet, rusty nails, and a delicate fern - a floss of green confetti. Then there was the little front room, with its low windows and damp wallpaper, cold through lack of use. Only at Christmas was a fire lit, or when a visitor had to be 'made welcome'. It was to this little room that some of the family of the *Treveal*'s crew came; to hear how their loved ones had been pulled from the sea or lost. In the cottage, Down the Lane, they had cottage hospitality and understanding.

I sat back down at the desk. The stale air was being sucked out of the open window and my head began to clear. I fingered the pile of papers on the desk: newspaper reports of the evidence given at the inquests and inquiry, and several short accounts of the disaster, and other material relating to it, which had been published over the years. The unrecorded, oral history I carried in my head would have to be measured against the documented history, and I realised that whatever else I did I would have to make sense of the evidence as reported in the summary and often contradictory newspaper accounts.

The Inquiry

The Board of Trade inquiry, under the Merchant Shipping Act 1894, into the loss of the *Treveal* was held at Weymouth on 5, 6, 7, 10, 11, 12 and 13 May 1920. The Report of Court was delivered on 19 May.

The Court consisted of Herbert John Groves, JP (President), and Oliver William Warner, JP. The judges were assisted by three naval assessors: Lieutenant J L Leftwich, RNR, Commander A S Houston, RNR, and Vice-Admiral O F Gillett, CB.

Mr J Pilcher, barrister, represented the Board of Trade, Mr W Cunliffe, barrister (instructed by Messrs Thomas Cooper & Co, London), represented the Shipowners, and Mr W Wilkinson, Admiralty law agent, Weymouth, represented the Admiralty. Commander H Innes observed the inquiry on behalf of the National Lifeboat Institution.

First Day - Wednesday, 5 May 1920 - Morning

MR PILCHER, in his opening statement for the Board of Trade, recalled the facts of the disaster and expressed respectful sympathy with the relatives of the men who lost their lives. He said the mishap was of a very disastrous character owing to the loss of life and the loss of a fine new ship. The Board of Trade viewed it with great concern and were determined to have a close inquiry into all the facts. The object of the inquiry, so far as the Board was concerned, was to find out, if possible, the cause of the stranding and of the subsequent loss of the ship and life.

It was not part of the Board's duty to make charges against any individual, although during the investigation the conduct of certain persons would come under the consideration of the court.

MR CUNLIFFE asked that the owners of the *Treveal* be made a party to the inquiry. He took that opportunity of expressing in public how deeply the owners regretted the loss of so many valuable lives - experienced, well-tried servants of the company. The owners sympathised with the relatives of the deceased in their great loss.

MR WILKINSON asked that the Admiralty also be made a party to the inquiry, and, on behalf of his clients, expressed sympathy with the relatives of the men who lost their lives.

(The Shipowners and the Admiralty were allowed by the court to become parties to the inquiry.)

MR PILCHER (continuing his address) said there were two parts to the inquiry. The court had to consider the cause of the stranding of the *Treveal*, and also the means which were available, some of which were put into use, for assisting the crew and the ship. Regarding the first part, there was very little evidence. Unfortunately, the master, who was on the bridge at the time, was among those who lost their lives. The principal witness would be the third officer; but the master being in charge, this officer was not responsible for the navigation. The second part was more complicated. There were three means by which assistance might be rendered: tugs, coastguards and lifeboats. There were tugs at Portland; there were coastguards at Lulworth, Kimmeridge, St Alban's and Swanage; and there were lifeboats at Weymouth, Swanage and Poole. Weymouth, the windward lifeboat, was launched, but unfortunately the summons was received too late for the lifeboat to be of any assistance. He drew attention to the methods of communication available: wireless, flags, telephones and rockets. Wireless messages were received as far distant as Rame Head (Plymouth), Portsmouth Dockyard and Dover. There was great activity, but unfortunately it was not successful. A curious point was that although the *Treveal* went aground at 9 o'clock on the night of 9 January, no signals of distress were made by her until 8 o'clock the following morning. Whether the crew thought they were safe or not he did not know. As late as 5.32 a.m. the *Treveal* sent a wireless signal to St Ives asking for salvage steamers and lighters. Regarding the weather, he observed that it grew worse towards morning, making signalling difficult and uncertain. He adverted to the fact that a tug, the *Pilot*, went out from Portland to search for the *Treveal*. The *Pilot* manoeuvred about for some time but failed to find her, even though the lights of the *Treveal* were burning all night. Regarding the *Treveal*'s movements before she went aground, he said she had called at Portland for a North Sea pilot, but none was available. After waiting an hour she proceeded up Channel, her course being set to carry her about four miles from St Alban's Head. It was, therefore, a mystery how she came to go ashore on Kimmeridge Ledge.

The clock struck midnight, the 75th anniversary of the *Treveal* disaster had passed, and I had begun the story - or rather, I realised, I had begun two stories: the story as told by the official inquiry, and my own telling of the story.

Having set this course, the official inquiry needs some explanation. It took place four months after the disaster and was intended to be the final word - after all the gossip and rumours, which invariably circulate following a shipwreck; and after, in the case of the *Treveal*, not one, but two inquests on the bodies of the dead, which, because of the limited scope of a coroner's investigation, had only served to intensify the existing debate and raise new questions besides. Public interest in the inquiry was considerable, and there was such a large gathering of officials, press and persons interested that during the first day a larger hall (the Sidney Hall) than the Weymouth Guild Hall was requisitioned by the court in order to provide the necessary accommodation.

The two judges (local magistrates) had the expert assistance of three naval assessors. The court allowed the Shipowners and the Admiralty to become parties to the inquiry, and as the 'long days of sitting' and examination of witnesses began, the inquiry settled into a regular rhythm: Mr Pilcher, for the Board of Trade, elicited a factual narrative from the witnesses; Mr Cunliffe, for the Shipowners, examined witnesses with a view to exposing shortcomings among those with a responsibility for rescue in the case of shipwreck; Mr Wilkinson, for the Admiralty, examined witnesses with a view to limiting the damage caused by Mr Cunliffe's examination; and the judges or assessors put questions to witnesses with a view to clarifying any outstanding matter.

My grandfather went down to Weymouth to give evidence on the second day of the inquiry. The only thing I ever heard about him and this aspect of the *Treveal* story was that he was chided by a fellow villager for describing himself only as a fisherman and not a 'Master Fisherman', which would have entitled him to a higher level of expenses.

Chapter 2

Twelve months and more passed during which I went painstakingly through the evidence given at the inquiry, as reported in half a dozen different newspapers, and made the first tentative steps to find out more about the crew of the *Treveal*.

I decided to visit St Ives, home of the Hain Steamship Company and nine of the crew, including Captain Charles Paynter. I drove down from Dorset early one foggy morning, wondering if there was anything more to learn about the company beyond what I already knew from two published accounts of its history: *The Story of the Hain Steamship Company*, by Sir George P Christopher, and *Hain of St Ives*, by K J O'Donoghue and H S Appleyard. As I approached Cornwall the fog grew worse, swirling around the car headlights like beckoning wraiths, and it was a relief to pull off the road and refresh myself with the plain facts of the Hain company's history over an equally straightforward breakfast.

The Hain family had been resident in St Ives for many generations:

> Their first recorded shipping venture would seem to be a part share in the fishing lugger DASHER, which was built and registered at St. Ives in 1816. Edward Hain (I), Michael Welch and Matthew Daniel, all described as mariners, took equal shares in the vessel. She was commanded by Edward Hain (I) ... The DASHER was successful, and on 17 February 1838 the schooner CAMILLA was purchased. This time control of the vessel was firmly in the hands of the Hain family, with 16 shares held by Edward Hain (I) and 32 shares held by his son Edward. The balance of the shares were held by Richard Paynter, a St. Ives fisherman whose family was closely connected with the Hains.
> (O'Donoghue and Appleyard, p 7)

In 1850 the Hains acquired a new schooner, *Mystery*. Edward Hain (II) took command of her and the *Camilla* was handed over to his son, the third Edward Hain. The business prospered in a small way over the next quarter of a century, with never more than three vessels in service at any one time. Thus might things have continued but for the ambition and enterprise of Edward Hain (IV).

Unlike his forbears, Edward Hain (IV) showed no inclination to go to sea. After an education in various private schools in St Ives, two years' training in accountancy and book-keeping at the local branch of Bolitho's Bank, and a spell at a tea-merchant's office in London, he returned to St Ives 'with a taste for bigger things, fired with a zeal thereto which frightened his father' (Christopher, p 8). The old man pondered the problem of -

> how to deal with this heartless and headstrong youth, who had threatened, with a stubbornness not to be appeased, to leave the family hearth and business if it was expected of him to remain merely to help manage those little sailing ships and whose ultimatum for continuing "under the flag" was the embarking into steamships or at least for the time being into one steamer.
>
> The youth's answer to the question where did he think the money was to be found for such madness was that it could be borrowed in the first instance from the Bolithos ...
>
> (Christopher, p 8)

O'Donoghue and Appleyard (p 9) give the following account of the pivotal moment in the company's history:

> The Bolithos were approached and took no time in deciding to support the venture by standing in with the money until a shareholding could be formed, and in agreeing to take shares themselves. Having secured financial support, young Edward visited the yard of John Readhead and Co. at South Shields, where a lasting relationship with the shipbuilders was formed. The first steamer was ordered and Readheads went on to build 73 more during Edward's lifetime ... one of the most outstanding owner/builder associations in British shipbuilding history.
>
> In recognition of the support provided by the Bolithos, the first steamer was named TREWIDDEN after the Bolitho estate outside Penzance. She was launched by the daughter of John Readhead on 26th November 1878 ... The shareholdings in this and subsequent early steamers were for the most part held by members of the Hain and Bolitho families, plus a large number of small investors from St. Ives and the neighbouring villages. There seemed to be no shortage of potential investors and an examination of early lists shows master mariners, farmers, mine agents and even local shopkeepers. This was to be the pattern of shareholding until the formation of the limited liability company in 1901.

The Hain Steamship Company Limited was registered on 16 September 1901. The fleet now comprised 22 steamships, and the company had offices in Cardiff and London, as well as in St Ives. The naming of the Hain ships had been standardised as long ago as the launch of the first steamer: all were named after Cornish farms, villages, or estates of prominent county families, and all had the prefix 'Tre', meaning 'homestead' or 'dwelling place'.

The personal and political life of Edward Hain (IV) blossomed as his company grew, and he would later become, in *Who Was Who*: 'HAIN, Sir Edward, Kt, *cr.* 1910 ... J.P. Cornwall and St. Ives ... *m.* 1882, Catherine, *d,* of James Hughes of Whitehaven, Cumberland; one *s.* one *d.* M.P. (L.U.) West (St. Ives) Cornwall, 1900-1906; President of the Chamber of Shipping of the United Kingdom, 1910-11; member St. Ives Town Council over 20 years, six times Mayor; 12 years member Cornwall County Council; Sheriff of Cornwall, 1912 ...' Meanwhile, the Hain fleet continued to expand at a phenomenal rate. By 1913 it numbered 36 ships, in addition to which another five were on order at Readheads: 'The rapid expansion prompted one shareholder to ask at an Annual General Meeting "Good God, where is the money coming from?" to which Sir Edward nonchalantly replied "That's just what we want to know!"' (O'Donoghue and Appleyard, p 10).

Edward Hain (IV)

19

Sir Edward suffered a severe blow in 1915 when his only son and prospective successor, Edward (V), was killed at Gallipoli in the Dardanelles campaign. He never fully recovered from the loss. In June 1917 he had a breakdown during a German air-raid on London, and returned home to St Ives to convalesce. He died on 20 September at Treloyhan Manor, the grand residence he had built for himself outside the town, leaving a personal fortune proved at £628,677 gross.

Lord Inchcape, on behalf of the P & O Steam Navigation Company, swiftly made an approach to the Hain board to ascertain if and on what terms the company was for sale: 'As a result of negotiations thus set on foot, the company's shares were purchased by the P. & O. Company, of which Lord Inchcape was chairman. With a judgment characteristic of that famous industrial chief, the management of the Hain company was left entirely in the hands of the men who had been trained in the Hain service ...' (Christopher, p 16). It was an appropriate posthumous accolade for Edward Hain (IV), who had transformed, almost single-handedly, a humble, provincial sailing ship business into a great industrial undertaking - one of the best-known trampship-owners in the world.

In the aftermath of the *Treveal* disaster, the company was discussed with great pride in the St Ives press. It was, in the *Western Echo* (17 January 1920), 'The Hain Line, with its always well-found and well-kept ships.' In the *St Ives Times* it was observed that, 'Among sailors the Hain Line has always enjoyed a good name' and that up until the First World War it had been 'remarkably free from casualties.' The Hain fleet was 'manned, officered and commanded in large part by Cornishmen. It was quite a common occurrence ... for the night train from St. Ives and neighbouring stations en route to contain a pretty high percentage of the personnel, from the master downwards, of a Hain steamer which would be signing-on in Cardiff ...' (Christopher, p 15). Mr Cunliffe, counsel for Hains at the inquiry into the loss of the *Treveal*, put it more eloquently still, in his closing speech to the court: 'the men who sailed in the Hain steamers were drawn very largely from the West of England, more especially St Ives, and the feeling between the company and their employees savoured more of friendship than anything else.'

The Inquiry
First Day - Wednesday, 5 May 1920 - Morning (continued)

ROBERT SAWLE READ (Managing Director of the Hain Steamship Company), examined by Mr Pilcher, gave formal evidence as to the ownership of the *Treveal*. His company owned 43 steamships. All their officers were personally known to him. Captain Paynter, the master of the *Treveal*, entered the company's service as a second mate in 1905. He was appointed temporary master in 1910, and permanent master in 1912. He was appointed to the *Treveal* in August 1919. He was an officer in whom they had absolute confidence. Mr Hutchinson, the first mate, had served during the war on convoy work, and had been a master's mate for a Cardiff firm.

Examined by Mr Cunliffe: The first intimation the Hain company had that the *Treveal* had gone ashore was a message received at 8 o'clock on the morning of 10 January. Witness immediately gave instructions to their London house to get in touch with the salvage agents, and instructed the company's marine superintendent to proceed to Swanage with discretionary powers.

By the Court: His company did not insure their ships with Lloyds. Any loss fell on the owners. The *Treveal* was under time charter to Messrs Brocklebank, of Liverpool, for 12 months at owner's risk. The owners had no interest in the cargo.

A Member of the Court: Did the captain try and get a pilot at Portland?
Witness: Yes.
The Member of the Court: He did not get one?
Witness: No.

(A telegram was produced, which was dispatched to the Hain company from Messrs Collins & Co (agents), Portland, stating that the *Treveal* had called at Portland for a North Sea pilot, but proceeded, as no pilot was awaiting her.)

The President: Was there no local pilot?
Witness: They wanted a North Sea pilot in connection with the mines.
By the Court: Hain vessels usually called at Deal for a pilot. When the weather was bad the captain would use his own discretion. The captain could have called at Plymouth had he so desired and obtained a pilot there. Their instructions were that the safety of the ships came first.

FREDERICK UREN (Marine Superintendent of the Hain Steamship Company), examined by Mr Pilcher, gave evidence as to the *Treveal*'s dimensions and specifications, and navigational, signalling and life-saving equipment. The *Treveal* was a good 10-knot ship.

(The vessel carried four lifeboats on davits, two on each side of the bridge deck. These boats were fully equipped according to Board of Trade Regulations. Each boat was capable of carrying 65 persons, one being sufficient for all the members of the crew. She had 6 lifebuoys and

21

57 lifebelts. She was provided with a patent sounding machine and log, and all other necessary equipment according to Board of Trade Regulations in regard to leads and lines. She had an electric Morse signalling lamp fitted on the bridge, distress and all other pyrotechnic signals. She had two compasses in position, the standard, a Lord Kelvin Compass on top of the wheel house by which the courses were set, and a Kelvin Compass in the wheel house by which the courses were steered. She was provided with a Marconi wireless apparatus, the operation room being abaft the wheel house on the bridge, and carried two operators. There was also a semaphore fitted on the bridge ... (Report of Court))

Examined by Mr Cunliffe: Captain Paynter was a friend. He was one of the best navigators, thoroughly experienced and reliable. The *Treveal*'s compasses were tested in September in the Clyde. (Deviation cards were produced, which had been taken from the chart room of the *Treveal* since the disaster.) Witness said he believed Captain Paynter kept these cards up to date. Captain Paynter was a most careful man. Witness stated that he was unable to board the *Treveal* until nine days after she stranded owing to the bad weather. He arrived at Chapman's Pool on 11 January. The *Treveal* had broken in two, the parts being 60 feet apart. Chapman's Pool was a most dangerous place in which to try to effect a landing without assistance from the shore.

Re-examined by Mr Pilcher: The deviation cards from the *Treveal* had been made up four months previously. Witness conceded that even the best compasses were liable to slight deviation, especially after a journey to the East.

By an Assessor: He could not find the log book of the *Treveal*. Possibly the log book and the rough log were taken by Captain Paynter when he left the ship and were lost.

The Assessor: How do you account for the vessel getting ashore where she did, coming from Portland, only a short distance?

Witness: I cannot understand it; it is beyond me.

(The Court adjourned for lunch.)

The fog had lifted and a bright sun was shining by the time I neared St Ives. There was one place I wanted to visit before reaching the town itself, and as soon as I found myself in what I guessed was its vicinity I stopped to ask directions.

'Could you tell me how to get to the old Hain manor house?'
A blank look.

'Sir Edward Hain's house?'
Still no response. I dug out O'Donoghue and Appleyard's book.
'Treloyhan Manor?'
'Ah, now ...' and directions followed.
Turning into the driveway of the house, a few minutes later, I hesitated on seeing a sign proclaiming it a Christian conference centre, but was fortified by another, with the universal invitation, 'Teas'.

Treloyhan Manor

Edward Hain built his magnificent residence - the equal of any great house of the county - in 1892, at Trelyon, a little village sitting high above St Ives and a world away from the old Hain house at Tregenna Terrace, in the town, where his forbears, master mariners in little sailing ships, had rubbed shoulders with their crews.

Edward Hain (IV)'s penchant for naming many of the ships of his fleet after the estates of county families, which began with the first steamer, is suggestive of a man possessed of the highest social ambitions, a suggestion reinforced by the naming of his house: Treloyhan Manor - the ancient spelling of Trelyon coupled with the word Manor suggesting, surely as it was intended to, a centuries old estate of rolling green acres, rather than a Victorian monument to the shifting of base cargoes at so much a nautical mile. In this 'ancestral home' the fine contents had not been accumulated over countless generations, but were bought in one great shopping spree. There were fine carpets, furniture and paintings; a beautiful bust of the Hains' young daughter, Grace, carved in marble by an Italian sculptor.

It lasted only a few decades. Today, the house, though little changed externally, is a shadow of its former self within. Anybody can drink a cup of tea in Sir Edward Hain's drawing room, and I doubt very much whether many of those who do know even the name of the former owner. I drove down into St Ives, thinking that perhaps in the town itself the memory of the once great Hain family would be more proudly preserved.

On my arrival, the harbourside was host to greedy seagulls, lobster pots and drying nets. Everywhere I looked jobbing builders were mending, patching, hammering and painting. Trades people were getting ready for 'the season': bright buckets and spades already cluttered the pavements, postcards hung in racks, and sticks of rock proclaimed St Ives to the world. My first thought on seeing the town was: how can so many shops, houses, stalls and cafes huddle together in such a small area? It was as if the hand of some angry god had once swept the buildings of the entire parish towards the sea, only to be merciful at the very last - leaving houses teetering above the surf and such novel sights, on the steep folds of land, as one man's cellar rising above his neighbour's attic. A fractured network of narrow, crooked streets, thoroughfares and alleyways, with granite setts and wide gutters, added to my disorientation: a street would suddenly narrow to a dead-end; a promising thoroughfare would twist and turn to a precipice of narrow steps; whilst the meanest looking alley might unexpectedly lead back to civilisation. The tower of the parish church, one of the tallest in Cornwall, reached up towards the terrace villas high above the harbour, but more striking, in a way, was the sheer number of Nonconformist chapels. Almost every corner I turned seemed to reveal another: Wesleyan, Primitive Methodist, Zion Congregational, Bible Christian. These, together with little signs, mounted at eye-level, which came relentlessly into a wanderer's vision, and which read 'Alcohol-free zone', struck a decidedly austere note in a town otherwise dedicated to welcoming hordes of summer visitors with all their vices and excesses.

In *An Historical Anthology of Bedford Road Chapel*, by David Allan, I had read about the strength of Methodism and teetotalism in old St Ives. Teetotalism came to St Ives in about 1838, the same year as the first Hain schooner, *Camilla*, was purchased. Within two years of a Teetotal Society being formed in the town it was reported that out of a population of less than 5,000 nearly 3,000 had signed the pledge: 'The Society's second Annual Report was a catalogue of success: "Almost the entire mining population of this parish are teetotallers, and out of the 88 vessels belonging to this port 74 ... sail without the use of the poisonous draught ... 44 of the masters are pledged members: upwards three 'fourths of the fishermen ..."' (Allan).

Continuing my first walk around St Ives, my mind wandered to the question: could alcohol have played a part in the *Treveal* disaster? 'They were all drunk' is a refrain which seems to follow a shipwreck as inevitably as a high tide follows a low. In the case of the *Treveal*, though, I had not detected even the slightest whiff of 'the poisonous draught', unless a Worth Matravers story, that some of the crew were wearing 'dancing pumps', could be taken as implying a certain gaiety, which might in turn suggest the consumption of alcohol. It was a link as tortuous as the streets of St Ives, and given the history of the town seemed inherently unlikely.

With time on my hands before my first appointment, at the museum, I made my way to the Bedford Road Chapel: the New Methodist New Connexion Chapel, opened in 1899, with the support of the Hain family: 'As a recognition of all that was done, it was resolved ... to invite Mr. Hain to open the Chapel door. The generosity and support of the Hain family did not stop when the Chapel was open ... it is recorded that Mrs. Hain offered to give the communion table, the chairs and the collection bags' (Allan). The opening of the chapel included 'the unveiling of "A Memorial Window" at the foot of which is the inscription "To the glory of God, and in loving remembrance of Grace, eldest daughter of Edward and Catherine S. Hain. Died June 23rd, 1898. Aged 15 years"' and at a luncheon after the opening, those who delivered short addresses included 'the Mayor of St. Ives (Mr. R. S. Read)' (*Methodist Evangelist*, No 9, Vol XIV, 1 September 1899, in Allan) - the managing director of the Hain company who gave evidence at the inquiry into the loss of the *Treveal*.

Turning into Bedford Road, I was greeted by the sight of a building which rivalled in size and grandeur the town's Anglican Church: it was in marked contrast to the many austere, democratic little chapels, with which, as I had already observed, St Ives was otherwise blessed. It was indeed a befitting place of worship for a man of Sir Edward Hain's wealth and social standing. Here, in the front pew, facing a beautiful pipe organ, played by Mr James Jacobs, a partner in the firm of W & J Jacobs, publishers of the *Western Echo*, sat Sir Edward and Lady Hain.

I asked the latter day minister of the Bedford Road Chapel, the Reverend Steven Wild, about the Hain connection. He doubted whether the chapel would ever have been built if it had not been for Hain money. He asked whether I had seen Treloyhan Manor. I said I had.

'Did you see the Hain safe there?'

'No, I didn't.'

'It's the biggest safe you've ever seen. You could eat your dinner in it.'

Back outside, in Bedford Road, I unfolded my town plan for the umpteenth time and charted a course to the St Ives Museum. Half an hour later, via a circuitous route which took in such streets as Atlantic Terrace, Virgin Street, Fish Street and Teetotal Street, I arrived at the foot of a flight of stone steps, which led to a door halfway up the face of a big, square building. The only reminder of the Hains I had seen en route was a dilapidated door bearing the Hain flag in a little back street.

I hoped for more from the museum, with its 'Hain Room'.

I was met by the curator, Mr Brian Stevens, and his wife, Margaret, a genial and hospitable couple whose generous assistance was to prove invaluable to me. Mr Stevens had gone to considerable lengths to have as much material as I might conceivably need readied in advance of my arrival. Piled on a table in the corner of the Hain Room were photographs, company ledgers, bound volumes of newspapers and names and addresses of people I might like to talk to.

Before delving into this mine of information, I refreshed myself with a cup of tea, courtesy of Mrs Stevens, and took in the exhibits on display in the Hain Room. There were photographs, paintings and models of ships, with the distinctive Hain colours: medium grey hull, yellow ochre main deck, white boat deck and black funnel with a large white 'H' on each side. There were photographs and paintings of Hain captains and senior officers of the company. Here was Robert Sawle Read. There was Sir Edward Hain. I drained my tea and turned to the table of materials in the corner of the room prepared for me by Mr Stevens.

I scanned the note on the top of the pile: 'Captain J Kemp MBE ... Captain Kemp is 92 and apart from a little hard of hearing ... is very alert in his mind ... He was an apprentice with Hains all those years ago ...' A St Ives address and telephone number were appended to the note.

Captain Kemp's house overlooked the wild Porthmeor Beach, on the other side of St Ives to the harbour. I was late for my appointment, having got lost coming from my guest house in the centre of town, and the old captain was standing in his porch, looking out for me when I arrived. He had an open, honest face and shook me warmly by the hand, gracefully accepting my apologies.

I sat down for tea and cake in his comfortable front room, where a painting of a Hain ship and a handful of exotic ornaments were a reminder of his long days of seafaring. Now, what did I want to know, he asked, and the interview began.

Q. I'm interested in the loss of the *Treveal* in 1920. I understand you were an apprentice with the Hain company at about that time?

A. I went to sea a year after she was lost. She was lost in January 1920 and I went to sea exactly 12 months later, and everybody in St Ives said, 'Hullo m'boy, you want to go to sea? I shouldn't go to sea.' (Laughs.) I went to sea and it was three years before I came home, in that ship (points to the painting on the wall), the *Trevessa*.

Q. What was it like being an apprentice with the Hain company?

A. We had to pay our rail fare to and from the ships, and all we got for four years was £45 indenture money. We had £5 the first year, £7 10s the second year, £12 10s the third year, and £20 the fourth year. We had to pay - my father had to pay - my fare to Belfast, and for all the clothes. But we had £5 for good conduct, or if we didn't run away. Your father had to pay a surety of £20, and that was in the 20s, the mid-20s.

Q. Was that the same for all the shipping companies?

A. Well, unless you joined Cunard, but your parents didn't have enough money to pay the surety money for Cunard.

Q. What was life aboard a Hain ship like at that time?

A. It all depended who you sailed with really. The food left something to be desired. I remember the cook one day - I was with old Captain Gibson when I was apprentice - and the cook made rock buns for Sunday afternoon. We was lying up Calcutta river then - we was up there waiting for a charter - and we boys we couldn't eat the buns, because they were so hard, that we were playing with them on the aft deck, bloody snowballs as it were. The chief steward had to go aft, to get his beef for next morning, and when he got aft he saw us boys throwing rock buns at one another and he went along and told Captain Gibson. Captain Gibson called us on along in the saloon and asked us who's throwing the buns around. Nobody admitted he was throwing the buns, so he says, 'All right, I'll punish you all.' So he kept us in the old gunners' quarters for three days on bread and water, and we didn't have no buns at all. So, we had some hard men in them days.

Q. Did the Hain company have any difficulty getting crews?

A. No. People used to, if they owed a lot of rent to Hains - Hains owned a lot of houses - they went there to pay their rents off, in the old days. That was the trouble in the old days. Hains would send perhaps eight men up from here all the way to Newcastle as ABs and when they got up there they found that the chief officer had already picked his crew and there was a fight outside the shipping office, the men wanting to kill the mate for picking his crew and the 'Bill' blaming the office down here for sending them all that way.

Q. How long were you with the Hain company?

A. I had 18 years with them and I was very glad to leave them. I left Hains and joined Andrew Weir (the Bank Line) and I was with Andrew Weir 32 years as master. I got an MBE from the Queen. I had to take over 7,000 people out of Colombo during the racial riots one night. Six ships we took there ... I was in Hains eight years with a master's ticket and only a second mate. I should have been master in Hains years, so I'd had enough and I joined Andrew Weir. I remember Captain Tullock came on the bridge one night in my watch and said, 'I see you come out of Hains's ships,' and I said, 'Yes, I have.' He said, 'Bloody hungry there, aren't they?' I said, 'I suppose they are.' But that was the only shipowners we knew.

Q. So was that the usual thing in the Hain company, for a second mate to hold a master's ticket?

A. (Laughing) I don't know about that. In the Blue Funnel line *all* the officers had to have a master's ticket, but in Hains - my brother Samuel was in the *Trevince* for his four years' apprenticeship and then when he went up for his exam - second mate - he failed in his eyesight: colour blind. He went back to Hains's offices down here and they said we can offer you a bosun's job, but we can't offer you an officer's job. We've just lost the *Treveal* and we're not taking any more uncertificated mates in our ships.

Q. Who told him that?

A. The company secretary, I think.

Q. William Cogar?

A. I think so; someone at the office down here.

Q. So the Hain company used to take uncertificated officers, before they lost the *Treveal*?

A. I did hear that there was an uncertificated officer on the bridge when she went ashore.

Q. On the bridge of the *Treveal*? Are you sure?

A. That's what I heard.

...

Q. Why do you think, in your case, Captain Kemp, that the Hain company kept you at second mate for so long with a master's ticket?

A. I was only a Boys School boy and I didn't have enough boyhood education as it were. I don't know. Someone did tell me once, 'You can't get on at Hains unless you're a Freemason.'

Q. Who told you that, do you remember?

A. It was just something I heard once. There was a Freemasons' room at Hains's offices, but I had no time for Freemasons.

...

Q. What was the Hain company's attitude towards alcohol? Did they have alcohol on the ships?

A. Only what was put aboard for Christmas or - You had a case of port, case of whisky, and a case of brandy ...

Q. So, if you were away at Christmas -

A. Yes, but it was only issued out as the master wished it to be. If you had a drunk master it was all bloody drunk before you left port.

Q. Robert Sawle Read, Hains' managing director, and Frederick Uren, the marine superintendent, gave evidence at the Board of Trade inquiry into the loss of the *Treveal*. Can you tell me anything about either of them?

A. Fred Uren died in the Second World War. They were inspecting the number three hold and the lunch bell happened to go and he sent the others to lunch and he fell down the hold.

I was sitting on the bed in my guest house in the silence of the middle of the night, with books, cuttings and notes spread everywhere. I'd had a nightmare, in which Frederick Uren had dragged me down into the hold as he fell. I'd woken in a cold sweat. It had been pitch black and I'd had no idea where I was. I'd stumbled across the sloping floor of the guest house room in a panic, imagining I was still aboard the ship of my nightmare, until, by chance, I'd bumped into a light switch. I'd been unable to sleep again afterwards.

What was I to make of the things I had seen and heard so far in St Ives? Captain Kemp's anecdote suggesting that Hain men were 'hungry' rang a bell somewhere and I searched through my papers until I found a letter from C Davies, who had a great uncle in the *Trewavas*, which went missing in 1892: 'I remember being told by my father when I was quite small, that the 'H' on the funnels of the steamers indicated 'hunger' - no doubt a malicious bit of tittle-tattle but with some degree of truth.' It occurred to me then that the same point had been made, though less colourfully expressed, in an objective appraisal of the company, found in the text of a submission by Lord Inchcape to the P & O directors when the purchase of the Hain line was under consideration: 'the steamers are worked on more economical lines than either the P & O or British India Companies, the ships being of a different class and their Captains, Officers and Engineers being less highly paid, and worked in as regards coal, repairs etc ...' (in O'Donoghue and Appleyard, p 119). What might generously be called the Hain company's 'thriftiness' was clear beyond a peradventure, but Captain Kemp had raised other matters, which led into altogether murkier waters: Freemasonry and uncertificated officers.

I'd got back to Mr Stevens at the museum after the interview to ask him about Freemasonry. He told me that Freemasonry was rife in shipping circles generally and that in the old days of sail many a skipper would actually fly a masonic flag: you see it in lots of old oil paintings of ships. He had no particular knowledge of Freemasonry in the Hain company.

What, legitimately, could be inferred? There was a Freemasons' room at the Hain offices, and such a set-up would have afforded Edward Hain (IV) and other senior members of the company a number of advantages in terms of the monitoring of prospective officers and captains. Managing director Robert Sawle Read was able to boast at the inquiry into the loss of the *Treveal* that the company owned 43 steamships and that 'All their officers were personally known to him.' In such a situation it would not be altogether surprising that the kind of whisper Captain Kemp heard would have circulated - whether it was factually accurate or not. Whatever the policies the Hain company adopted in the promotion of its officers, they do seem to have resulted in the loss of at least some good men, judged by the experience of Captain Kemp; but, ultimately, the company can only really be criticised if, conversely, the policies allowed on to the bridges of their ships men of a lesser talent or character than those who had to go elsewhere to have their abilities recognised. While post-World War I, the company having lost its share of masters and mates - to brass-cased shell, bobbing mine, or 'nerves' - the situation may have been ripe for hasty, 'who-you-know-not-what-you-know' promotions, I had seen no evidence that such promotions were ever made, either generally, or in the particular case of the *Treveal*.

What of the other matter raised by Captain Kemp - uncertificated officers? Employing uncertificated officers would be consistent with the Hain company's thriftiness; and perhaps also with its particular history. In the early days of the company there were no examinations of competency for masters and mates. Certificates became obligatory for foreign-going merchant officers only with the passing of the Mercantile Marine Act 1850, and for masters and mates of home-trade vessels with the passing of the Merchant Shipping Act 1854. The Hains at that time - pre-Edward Hain (IV) - were still operating only a tiny fleet of sailing ships. In this decade of regulation, Edward Hain (II) retired from seafaring and came ashore to manage the fleet, and his son, Edward (III), had to produce evidence that he had commanded vessels for several years in order to be granted a Certificate of Service - obviating the need to pass a formal examination. It is not difficult to imagine how the introduction of certificates of competency was viewed by the kind of small, independent company that Hains then was. The owners were captain's of their own ships and knew every man jack of their crews. What could a piece of paper tell them that close observation of how a man worked and handled himself at sea couldn't?

For whatever reasons, the Hain Steamship Company was less fussy than some other companies about certificates, and from what Captain Kemp had said, did not always require a certificate at all for their third officers. (It was not a *legal* requirement: there was no third mate's examination, and in order for him to be certificated he had to have passed a second mate's examination.) But did any of this have any relevance to the loss of the *Treveal*? According to Captain Kemp, 'Yes': he had heard there was an uncertificated officer on the bridge when she went aground. According to the evidence, however, 'No'. Mr Cunliffe, counsel for the Hain company at the inquiry into the loss of the *Treveal*, in his closing speech to the court, stated unequivocally that he thought: 'the court would be satisfied from the evidence that the captain and officers were experienced, trustworthy, and *certificated* men.' (My emphasis.) Furthermore, an entry in one of the Hain ledgers at the St Ives Museum pertaining to the appointment of William Donald as the *Treveal*'s third officer (and it can only be to Donald that the 'uncertificated' allegation referred) carefully records, not only the period of his service and the capacity in which he served, but, specifically, that he was an 'Ex-apprentice Trevethoe, holding 2nd Mate's ticket.' If there is, perhaps, a suspicion that the Hain company 'doth protest too much' - it was not the usual practice in the company's ledgers for any mention to be made of what certificate any particular officer held - the evidence, at the end of the day, seemed to be for the company and against the rumour Captain Kemp had heard.

The light of dawn was now creeping into the guest house room and I closed my eyes, all the evidence going round and round in my head like a bronze propeller. I remembered once having been told that sometimes a ship's propeller would not be quite 'true', causing it to 'sing' (vibrate), and that if that happened the ship had to be dried out, and the strongest man, with the biggest hammer, had to give it an almighty thump. Anxiously wondering if my subconscious was suggesting some kind of analogy with the evidence, I drifted into a fitful sleep.

Chapter 3

I had expected my visit to St Ives to be a brief one - a couple of days - but it was soon clear that I would need to extend it: there were more people to see and places to visit; and, at the museum, the pile of material on the table was only slightly less mountainous than on the day I arrived. Mrs Stevens arranged for a photograph of the *Treveal* - the only photograph of the ship where she isn't split in two - to be copied for me, and the pile went down by about $^1/64$ inch.

I had been used to thinking of the *Treveal*, as in the many other photographs, as a wreck; but to gaze upon her whole was to remember that God's blessing had once been asked for her and all who sailed in her. Had God forsaken her and her crew even as she was launched? Had some keel-hauled gremlin already claimed her for a plaything?

SS Treveal

The *Treveal* (official number 142573) was originally ordered by His Majesty's Government as a First World War 'Liberty' type vessel. She was laid down at the yard of Caird & Company, Glasgow, in 1918, and was to have been named *War Jonquil*, but the war ended before she was completed, and she was acquired - together with another 15 wartime standard ships - by the Hain company, as part of the post-war rebuilding of its fleet. She was fitted out by Harland & Wolff, Glasgow, and was launched in September 1919. She was the second ship of the Hain line to bear the name *Treveal* (a modified spelling of Trevail - a hamlet between Zennor and St Ives), the first *Treveal* having been torpedoed and sunk by a German submarine off the Skerries, Anglesey, in February 1918. *Treveal* (II) was 400 feet in length, her gross tonnage was 5,243 tons (registered tonnage 3,226 tons) and she was built to carry dry cargo. She had a crew of 43 and no passenger accommodation. She was, as Hains' marine superintendent, Frederick Uren put it at the inquiry, 'a good 10-knot ship' - in which respect she fell squarely within the parameters marked out in one of the late Sir Edward Hain's favourite enjoiners upon his staff: 'Don't forget, we are cart horses, not race horses' (in Christopher, p 16). In the Report of Court following the inquiry into her loss, the *Treveal* was found to have been 'exceptionally well fitted and found in every respect.' If the Hain company was known for keeping its costs low, it does not appear that they cut corners with the ships themselves.

So much for the *Treveal*. What of her captain, Charles Paynter? On my arrival in St Ives, I knew very little about him, beyond what had been said in evidence at the inquiry: he was an officer in whom the Hain company had 'absolute confidence' (Robert Sawle Read), and he was 'one of the best navigators, thoroughly experienced and reliable ... a most careful man' (Frederick Uren). I had asked Mr Stevens, at the museum, before my visit, if he could keep a particular eye out for anything relating to Captain Paynter, but Mr Stevens had informed me when I arrived that he was proving 'a very elusive captain'. However, things had improved since my arrival and information on him was growing steadily.

I had scoured the bound volumes of the two local newspapers - the *St Ives Times* and the *Western Echo* - at the museum. The *St Ives Times* (16 January 1920) was the first to publish details about Captain Paynter's background following the disaster:

> Capt. Chas. Paynter, the master of the Treveal, was one of the most popular skippers of the line. Mr. R. S. Read said he was a very competent master, and one who had been particularly free from casualties. It is a fact that he was at sea the whole course of the war, commanding one ship or another, and never had a single mishap. "He did not suffer from nerves," remarked Mr. Read,

"and always went to sea. This was his first mishap, I believe, and I am sorry to say it was fatal." The owners had such an opinion of his capabilities that the Treveal was not the first new boat he had been given command of. He had been fifteen years with the Hain Line, previous to which he served on Chellew boats ... He was unmarried, and was a member of the Tregenna Lodge of Freemasons.

In a further paragraph in the same edition of the *St Ives Times* it was noted that -

Captain Charles Paynter, master of the Treveal, was the son of the late Mr. Thomas Paynter and of the late Mrs. Nicholls, of 5, Barnoon Terrace, St. Ives, who died in December, 1916. Captain Paynter leaves three sisters, Mrs. J. B. Walker and the Misses Carrie and Lizzie Paynter the two latter of whom he has made his home with. Whilst of a retiring disposition he was very popular with those with whom he came in contact, and in the many letters of sympathy received by the family high tributes are paid, not only to his personal character, but to his efficiency and consideration as a Captain.

Mr Stevens in the meantime had transcribed Captain Paynter's complete record of employment with Hains from the company ledgers:

Capacity	Steamer	Date of Appointment	Date of Leaving
2nd Mate	Tregothnan	Jan 4 1905	July 20 1905
1st Mate	Trevessa	Aug 4 1905	Sept 26 1906
do.	Trevelyan	Oct 3 1906	Aug 3 1910
Master	do.	Aug 3 1910	Oct 25 1910
Master	Trefusis	Nov 1 1910	Jan 15 1911
1st Mate	Treneglos	Feb 28 1911	July 4 1912
Master	do.	July 5 1912	Sept 25 1912
Master	Tresillian	Oct 1 1912	Apr 14 1914
Master	Tregarthen	May 27 1914	Aug 24 1917
Master	Trewidden	Aug 28 1917	June 19 1919
Master	Treveal	Aug 28 1919	Jan 10 1920

The amiable curator had also transcribed for me a report which had appeared in the *Western Echo* (16 December 1916):

Death. Nicholas. December 9th at 5 Barnoon Terrace, St. Ives. Mrs Caroline Nicholas, aged 69 years.
After a long illness, Mrs Caroline Nicholas passed away on Friday last at 5 Barnoon Terrace. Much sympathy is extended to her daughters, Mrs J B Walker and the Misses Carrie and Lizzie Paynter, and to her son, Captain Charles Paynter, of SS Tregarthen. The funeral on Tuesday, was conducted by the Rev. G M Webster B.A. The chief mourners being, Mrs J B Walker, Misses Carrie and Lizzie Paynter, (daughters) Mrs J Grenfell, (sister) Messrs T and I Pearce, (brothers) Mr J B Walker, (son-in-law) Mrs Chard, Mrs Bosanquet, Mrs Craze, (nieces) Captain Hollow and Captain J Grenfell, (brother-in-laws) Mrs T Pearce, (sister-in-law). A large number of other relatives and friends attended to pay a fond tribute of respect.

I walked up to see the house at Barnoon Terrace which had been the home of the Paynters for more than 20 years. In Captain Paynter's day the terrace had exuded a distinct air of gentility, and his neighbours included the aforementioned James Jacobs, organist and choirmaster at the Bedford Road Chapel, and partner in the firm of W & J Jacobs, publishers of the *Western Echo*. The Jacobs' home was the centre of the musical life of St Ives, and for many years was the headquarters of a local string orchestra. Standing on a lofty height above the town, the ground falling away so sharply that one could almost reach out and touch the tops of the buildings below, the commanding views of the bay and sea approaches to the port had also made the terrace popular with those who had a vested interest in the sea-ways. Mr Stevens had told me:

I have often during my researches been amazed by the great number of sea captains who had occupied the houses, and thought how much of their time, when home from trips or in retirement, they spent looking to seawards. This with spy glass and note book handy, to record whatever might interest them or the shipping circles with which they were connected. Young Charles had many such masters living in Barnoon Terrace during his formative years, and perhaps with also family connections this led him on to a seafaring career.

I stood outside Captain Paynter's house pondering this. For all the knowledge I had acquired, he remained 'an elusive captain' in my mind. When he had stood on the bridge of the *Treveal* at the start of her maiden voyage, he had been 41 years old: he had been sailing the oceans of the world for a quarter of a century, and had enjoyed a faultless career. Yet still I could not 'see' him and wondered about his formative years.

I came into the St Ives Museum one morning and on top of the pile of material on the desk in the corner sat an unfamiliar photograph. Mr Stevens appeared and explained: 'Picture of Captain Paynter. I've been talking to his great niece.' I took a deep breath and picked it up. A head-and-shoulders portrait. Not in his captain's uniform. My first thought was: 'He doesn't look like a captain; he looks like a well-to-do shopkeeper.' He was, I thought, a steady, serious-looking man, and a man who had 'got on' - done well for himself.

Charles Paynter

Three days later I sat down in my guest house room to piece together what I could of Charles Paynter's background and history. I had visited his great niece, Mrs Elizabeth Beach, who had never known her great uncle Charles, but who kindly showed me the big family Bible, inscribed with the names and dates of birth of Paynter children going back to the 1700s, various birth and marriage certificates, and a Freemason's medallion, which had belonged to Captain Paynter's brother-in-law, James B Walker; I had spoken on the telephone to Mrs Caroline Brassington, the second of four Walker children, who was seven years old at the time of Captain Paynter's death; I had been to see the records of the Zion Congregational Church, courtesy of the Reverend Ian Densham, where Captain Paynter's parents married, and I had extracted various details from census returns and old post office directories.

Charles Paynter's early years were not spent at elevated Barnoon Terrace, but down below, in the busy cramped streets at sea level. He was born on 12 November 1877 in Fore Street, a narrow, crooked thoroughfare - but the principal commercial street of the town - close by the harbour. His father, Thomas Simon Paynter, was a grocer. Thomas's father, John, had died when Thomas was a boy, and Thomas had started work in the family shop at a tender age. He seems to have devoted himself largely to the business, only taking a wife - Caroline Pearce, ten years his junior - when middle age was upon him. Caroline was a daughter of Isaac Pearce, who had a butcher's shop a few doors away from the Paynters' grocery. Thomas and Caroline were married on 14 March 1877 in the Zion Congregational Church. Charles was their first child. For some reason, perhaps because he was born eight months after the marriage, his parents did not have him baptised in the Zion chapel. It would not have aroused a great deal of comment: there has always been a certain amount of more or less gratuitous toing and froing between the various chapels in the town (the *Treveal*'s carpenter, Peter Cogar, for example, was baptised in the Zion chapel, but was a Primitive Methodist at the time of his death). Whatever the circumstances of Charles's conception, or his parents' marriage, his paternal grandmother, Elizabeth, who was still alive - she was 80 years old and living with the family when he was born - must have been thrilled to have survived long enough to witness the arrival of an heir to the little grocery business. Three more children - the girls, Honor, Caroline and Elizabeth - were born in quick succession.

Thomas Paynter, like his father before him, died when his children were young. However, Charles was not put immediately into harness in the family business by his widowed mother, as Thomas had been by his, but continued his schooling. He was a boy in a house of women, raised on the hard benches of Nonconformism, and must have felt his responsibility and duty to his family acutely in that milieu. Was it, perhaps, because of this that he never took on the additional 'burden' of a wife? Or was he of the same ilk as another captain, Captain Edward Reed, foreman of the jury at the coroner's inquests on the victims of the *Treveal* disaster, who said that he would never marry, 'unless to a lady'? Whatever the reason, his life was to be largely spent in an all-male preserve. He would skipper cargo steamers, not luxurious passenger liners. There would be no holding sway at the Captain's Table: no chortling with a wealthy old dame; no tickling the chin of a chubby-cheeked damsel. Instead, just the company of men and the toil of moving great quantities of raw materials around the world.

In going to sea, Charlie Paynter broke the line of continuity established by his shopkeeping forbears, as surely as his bachelorhood would ensure the death of the Paynter name in his branch of the family. His chosen career was not, however, entirely alien to his kinsfolk. There were numerous salty relatives in the wider family: two of his mother's sisters were married to sea captains (John Grenfell, who had married Honor Pearce, and who was a near neighbour, may have been a particular influence on the young, fatherless Charlie), and there were Paynters - of his father's and grandfather's generations - who were fishermen, master mariners and shipwrights.

Of Charles Paynter's early career at sea I knew nothing, except that previous to joining the Hain line as a second mate in 1905 'he served on Chellew boats.' In the Hain company the Paynter name was well known, being the name of the only non-Hain shareholder in the family's first schooner, as well as the maiden name of Edward Hain (IV)'s mother. Although Charles Paynter was not of the same branch of the family, it was not a bad name to have for an officer looking to 'get on' at the company. At some point he joined the Tregenna Lodge of Freemasons, and, if he had any sense at all, he would also have switched his spiritual allegiance to the new Bedford Road chapel - the Hain church. He may well have done so: his brother-in-law, James Walker, as well as being a prominent local tradesman and Freemason, was a prominent figure in the chapel; and certainly, as time went on, and Chief Officer Paynter became a temporary master, then a permanent master, it is easy to imagine the genteel family - Mr and Mrs Walker, Captain Paynter and the Misses Carrie and Lizzie, perhaps accompanied by their mother when her deteriorating health permitted (she had remarried - to a man called Nicholls or Nicholas, who neither Mrs Beach nor Mrs Brassington could tell me anything about - but been widowed again) - walking down from Barnoon Terrace to the ostentatious chapel at Bedford Road, in preference to one of the other chapels, which, in comparison, were small, cold and dark.

The Hain company could surely have asked for no more hard-working and dedicated a servant than Captain Charles Paynter. His spells at home between voyages were typically brief and he stood the heavy strain of the war years so well that at no time did he return home with 'nerves'. Indeed, his dedication was such that he was at sea - in the *Tregarthen*, carrying timber - during the last 'long illness' of his mother; he was at sea when she died, on Friday, 9 December 1916, and when she was buried four days later. Mrs Brassington recalled that as a very young girl she sat for long hours 'at Ma's [her grandmother's] bedside, with a bell to ring' in case of emergency. Of her Uncle Charles she remembered little: 'When he came home from sea, he would give us children shiny sixpences', but he was away such a lot and for such long periods that, at the age she then was, she 'did not really notice when he never came home at all.'

The Inquiry
First Day - Wednesday, 5 May 1920 - Afternoon

WILLIAM DONALD (Third Officer of the *Treveal*), examined by Mr Pilcher, gave evidence of the ship calling at Portland and proceeding on her voyage.

(Witness said the *Treveal* arrived off Portland at about 6 p.m. on Friday, 9 January. Captain Paynter applied to the Admiralty by signal for a pilot. The reply was that there was no pilot available, but letters would be sent in an hour if they would care to wait. As far as witness knew, no other message was received. They waited and a boat came off with the letters. They sailed at 7.43 p.m. ... A Juror wanted to know whether the witness thought the catastrophe would have happened if there had been a pilot aboard the vessel. *The Coroner*: I don't think I can put that question. It is a matter of opinion. (Inquest))

Witness said he came on the bridge at 8 p.m. Captain Paynter was on the bridge and told him to steer SE by E$1/2$E by compass, saying that would be SE by E (magnetic). At 8.07 p.m. the Shambles light was abeam. The captain told him it was two miles distant and the course SE by E $1/2$ E was continued. The compasses had been checked daily. On the night of the wreck there was a fresh wind blowing from WSW, it was raining and visibility varied. At 8.45 p.m. witness told Captain Paynter he thought he saw the loom of land half a point on the port bow, but the captain told him he was mistaken. He repeated his statement to the captain, who then told him to alter course half a point to the southward. Shortly afterwards the vessel struck. The engines were put full speed astern, but the ship remained fast. Captain Paynter ordered the ship's lifeboats to be got ready as a precaution.

(They communicated with Portland by wireless, asking for assistance, about 9.15 p.m. Witness could not say if there was a reply. A tug was asked for. Wireless signals for tugs were continued and a message was received at 12.15 a.m. that a tug, *Pilot*, was leaving from Portland. No tug appeared. (Inquest))

Between 12 and 1 a.m. they communicated with the coastguard at St Alban's Head by Morse lamp, giving the name of their ship, their position, and asking if there was a safe landing inshore. A reply was received that there was a good landing straight in, but that they had better wait until daylight. They did not ask for assistance from the coastguards. Shortly before daylight, between 7 and 7.30 in the morning, they saw the lights of the tug or some vessel. She was about one and a half to two miles away on their starboard beam. They signalled 'Are you the tug?' but got no reply. They then signalled to her to stand in closer, but saw no result. The weather was then thicker. At 5.30 in the morning witness did not consider there was any danger to life. They did not think then that the ship was going to break up. At 8 o'clock they sent out signals of distress and a message that they were about to abandon ship. So far as witness knew, no answer was received. The coastguards at St Alban's Head made no reply. The tug was in sight but appeared to make no movement towards them. The ship was then creaking ominously and appeared to be breaking up. Their starboard lifeboats were carried away, and huge seas sweeping over them threatened to swamp the port boats. They abandoned ship in the two port lifeboats at about 9 o'clock. There were 22 men in the captain's boat, and 21 in the chief officer's. The captain was the last to leave the ship. Lifebelts had been put on. Both boats got well away. They got between 50 and 100 yards of the shore when the boat witness was in capsized and they were thrown into the water. Witness clambered back on to the upturned boat, and helped the chief officer and boatswain regain their hold. Two others also got to the boat. Finding that the boat was not making towards the beach, witness thought he would try and swim for it. He reached the shore with the assistance of the Reverend Piercy and Mr Lander. There appeared to be nobody else on the beach. Witness said he crawled up to a house, and found there were three men there before him.

Examined by Mr Cunliffe: The tug could have brought a lifeboat close to their ship. Some attempt was made at signalling on the tug, but they could not read the signals either through the thickness of the weather or the poor lamp on board the tug. If the ship's boats could have been helped by a rope from the shore they would have got in. He did not see a member of the coastguard until between 2 o'clock and 2.30 in the afternoon. It was the habit of Captain Paynter to instruct his officers to check the deviation book. Lights were burning on the *Treveal* all through the night.

Examined by Mr Wilkinson: When the coastguards at St Alban's Head signalled that there was safe landing at Chapman's Pool there would have been no danger in landing there. The weather got worse afterwards. There might have been coastguards on the beach before 2 o'clock and he not have seen them. Witness stood by his opinion that the tug could have towed a lifeboat close to the ship: in fact, he saw no reason why the tug itself could not have got round astern and taken them off.

An Assessor put it to the witness that the course from Portland could not have been correct.

Witness said they must have been further away from the Shambles than was thought by the captain.

Re-examined by Mr Pilcher: When the crew abandoned ship they had no idea their lives would be in danger: they did not anticipate there would be any difficulty in the operation of landing. Witness thought they were justified in leaving the ship. Their lives would have been in danger had they stayed on board. Captain Paynter did not think it necessary to fire signals of distress during the night. So far as witness knew, no SOS wireless signal was sent out before daylight.

One morning, after what had become my usual early stroll around the harbour, I returned to my guest house for breakfast. There was some post for me. I took the bundle, which had been forwarded on to me from Dorset, up to my room, reading the postmarks - Cornwall, South Wales and London - as I climbed the stairs, and banging my head against a low beam, which never failed to catch me out. The London parcel, a hefty cardboard tube, also bore the legend, 'National Maritime Museum', and would contain copies of William Donald's certificates of competency. The other letters, I guessed, would be responses to letters I had written to the *West Briton* newspaper, which had a wide Cornish readership, and the *South Wales Evening Post*, requesting information. I had received a good response to an earlier letter published in the *St Ives Times*, and had decided to repeat the exercise in the hope of discovering more about, on the one hand, the Cornish members of the crew who did not come from St Ives, and, on the other, Third Officer Donald and Chief Engineer Thirkell, who came from Swansea and Cardiff respectively.

I opened the single letter with a Welsh postmark first: 'I am the only son of William John Donald referred to. Sadly my father died in tragic circumstances in 1936 but I have a vague recollection of the sinking of the S.S. Treveal and stories which have passed down through our family which may be of interest to you ...' There was a photograph of William Donald enclosed. He looked a hearty, easy-going sort of man. I put the letter and photograph to one side, with the parcel from the National Maritime Museum, and turned to the three remaining letters.

The first was from Frank Argall of Truro, a nephew of Frederick Argall, one of the *Treveal* apprentices, and a photograph of Frederick was enclosed. The second was from Richard Nettley of Helston, informing me that Frederick Argall's brother, Charles, was still alive and that he had sent my letter in the *West Briton* newspaper on to him. The third was from Charles himself, writing from his son's home in Plymouth. He would be returning to his own home in Middlesex in a few days if I would like to contact him when he got back.

I turned my attention back to William Donald. In the story of the *Treveal* disaster the first mate (Edwin Hutchinson) and the second mate (Charles Tait) are little more than shadows. They were not on the bridge when the *Treveal* stranded, they were both drowned in Chapman's Pool, and in the evidence of witnesses at the inquiry they played no significant part in the events of the long night until Chief Officer Hutchinson emerged on the morning of 10 January to take charge of the second lifeboat when the crew abandoned ship. In the circumstances it is sufficient to observe that the chief officer was a 43-year-old West Country man; that, according to the Hain ledgers in the St Ives Museum, it was his first voyage with the company; and that, according to Robert Sawle Read, 'Mr Hutchinson ... had served during the war on convoy work, and had been a master's mate for a Cardiff firm.' Second Officer Tait, who was 22, came from West Hartlepool, and a previous appointment with Hains is detailed in the ledgers: second mate of the *Trevanion*, 3 November 1918 to 9 July 1919.

If the *Treveal*'s first and second officers were notable largely by their absence, Third Officer Donald was one of the most prominent figures in the whole affair. Not only was he on duty when the *Treveal* went aground, but he got through the terrible ordeal of the following morning to become the only surviving witness of events on the bridge, before, as, and after the ship stranded. Furthermore, his subsequent history, I would discover later, seemed persistently to hark back to the loss of the *Treveal* and to raise unexpected questions. But that was all in the future. I was then concentrating on trying to clear up the business of whether Donald was, or was not, certificated when he sailed in the *Treveal*, before I spoke to his son. I first extracted his career with the Hain company from his applications to be examined for certificates of competency. I noticed that he had carried on with Hains after the loss of the *Treveal*, which was new information to me, Mr Stevens, at the museum, having extracted from the ledgers, at my request, only his pre-*Treveal* career. I put the dates from the ledgers in brackets alongside the dates given in the examination applications, in case of any discrepancies which might bear on the certification question:

Capacity	Steamer	Date of Appointment	Date of Leaving
Apprentice	Trevethoe	Sept 18 1914	Sept 18 1918
	(Indenture date: Sept 18 1914)		
3rd Mate	Trevethoe	Sept 18 1918	June 16 1919
3rd Mate	Treveal	Sept 6 1919	Jan 10 1920
		(Sept 4 1919	Jan 10 1920)
3rd Mate	Tremorvah	June 16 1920	Aug 25 1921
2nd Mate	Trevanion	Feb 9 1922	Mar 22 1922
2nd Mate	Lena	May 16 1922	Nov 28 1922
2nd Mate	Lena	Dec 2 1922	June 29 1923

Having passed his master's examination in 1923, there were no further applications to be examined and, therefore, no further details of William Donald's career. He was still with the Hain company in 1923 - the *Lena* being a ship managed by Hains on behalf of the Mercantile Steam Ship Company.

From the papers from the National Maritime Museum and some brief details of William Donald's life contained in the letter from his son, I tried to put his early career in context, before turning to the certification question.

William John Donald was born at Swansea on 29 October 1898 and was the son of a sea captain. His mother outlived her husband - and went on to outlive two more, both of whom were also mariners. In September 1914, at the age of 15, Donald joined the Hain company as an apprentice in the *Trevethoe*. That his apprenticeship coincided with the First World War, and that he acquitted himself admirably during what were dangerous and demanding years for any sailor, let alone a lad of his age, is clear enough. He received the Mercantile Marine war service medal, but more significantly, on 18 September 1918, at the age of 19, he was appointed third officer of the *Trevethoe*. A year later, he joined the *Treveal*.

William Donald

My impression was that Donald was a rising star in the Hain company, an impression supported by an inspection of his application to be examined for a certificate of competency as a second mate. The form was filled out in a flowing, confident hand, and was signed with the casual, unextravagant flourish of a man who knew exactly who he was and where he was going. In the section 'Personal Description of Candidate' his complexion was recorded as 'fresh'. Perhaps tellingly, that youthful epithet would never again appear on any of his subsequent applications, although he was no older than 22 when he sat his first mate's examination, and 24 when he was examined for his master's ticket.

But did Donald have his second mate's ticket when he sailed in the *Treveal*? His date of appointment was either 4 September 1919 (according to the Hain ledgers) or 6 September (according to his own later application to be examined for his first mate's certificate). Nothing seemed to me to turn on the discrepancy. Donald submitted his application to be examined on 21 August 1919, was examined on 25 August, and certified passed by the examiner on 27 August - all before his date of appointment (whether 4 or 6 September) as third mate in the *Treveal*. Yet, I was unsure when Donald was *issued* his certificate. The papers included a copy of a 'Certificate of Competency' granted 'By Order of the Board of Trade, this 1st day of September 1919' and a copy of another paper, perhaps the *verso* of that just mentioned, stating that the certificate was 'Issued at the Port of Cardiff on the 24th day of September 1919.' Donald was certainly a certificated officer when the *Treveal* went aground, but it appeared to me that he may not have been (or, rather, that he had still to receive notification) when Hains appointed him. What was certain was that prior to joining the *Treveal* he had sailed as an uncertificated third mate in the *Trevethoe*. It seemed, then, to have been the Hain company's sheer good fortune that they avoided the embarrassment of the *Treveal* going aground with an uncertificated third mate on the bridge. Little wonder, I thought, that Captain Kemp had heard the rumour he did.

I looked out of my guest room window. The washing lines strung across the street like a ship's rigging, which had been full of drying clothes when I had last looked out, were now empty, and the day was drawing to its close. I went downstairs to the payphone, with a pocket full of coins, and dialled the number which would connect me with Malcolm Donald, the son of the *Treveal*'s precocious third officer. There was no reply.

Among the several time-worn photographs of the *Treveal* broken in half on Kimmeridge Ledge, there is one taken from a passing excursion steamer - perhaps the steamer whose engineer used to leave his upturned greasy cap outside the engine room door with a small card reading, 'Don't forget the engineer.' Chief Engineer Robert Thirkell, a long-standing servant of the Hain company, was the only one of the *Treveal*'s engineers to survive. I had received no correspondence relating to him, but he left a colourful self-portrait, telling his story more frequently, dramatically and bitterly than any other survivor. In addition to his testimony at the official inquiry, the press had the privilege of an interview with him in the immediate aftermath of the disaster, the owners had the benefit of a letter giving his forceful views on how so many lives came to be lost, and the Tennant Lodge of Freemasons, at Cardiff, had 'the extreme pleasure of welcoming Bro. R. H. W. Thirkell after his miraculous escape from death in the s.s. Treveal,' and of hearing 'a very vivid account of his terrible experiences ...' (*St Ives Times*, 13 February 1920).

When he first stepped into the gleaming new engine room of the *Treveal*, Chief Engineer Thirkell can hardly have imagined that disaster lay but a few short months away. The *Treveal* may have been a 'cart horse', but compared to some of the old tubs an engineer of his longevity must have met with in his time, she was a ship he must almost have felt he could have sailed to the moon and back, given enough coal and men to shovel it. Although he would later fire off criticism in many directions, he had 'no complaint to make about the *Treveal* or her equipment.' One of the few other beneficiaries of his praise was Captain Charles Paynter.

The two men had several things in common, beyond just age and rank. They were both 'company men', having spent the best parts of their careers with the Hain line; they were both Freemasons; and they both appear to have been bachelors (Paynter certainly was; Thirkell was as far as a man who sailed with him afterwards knew). The engineers' ledgers in the St Ives Museum were not as detailed as the officers', but a comparison of Captain Paynter's record with Thirkell's (which read 1st Engineer - May 1 1903 Trevelyan; Feb 18 1907 Trevider; Nov 2 1909 Treveal [I]) raised the possibility that they had been to sea together on a previous occasion to the *Treveal* - in the *Trevelyan* in 1906/7.

It is not known what Captain Paynter thought of Chief Engineer Thirkell, but Thirkell's admiration of, and loyalty to the captain come across very clearly. In an interview with the press, 24 hours after the tragedy, the chief engineer stated that: 'He admired the great ability of Capt. Paynter, his handling of the wreck situation, and the splendid manner in which he and his men without exception stood by the ship till the last' (*St Ives Times*, 16 January 1920). Thirkell would later qualify the second part of this statement when examined at the inquiry. Indeed, he said much which he later had to qualify or retract, or which was otherwise proved incorrect. The most outspoken of the *Treveal* survivors, his evidence was not always the most reliable.

The Inquiry
First Day - Wednesday, 5 May 1920 - Afternoon (continued)

ROBERT THIRKELL (Chief Engineer of the *Treveal*), examined by Mr Pilcher, said he had no complaint to make about the *Treveal* or her equipment. Witness gave evidence of the ship calling at Portland and proceeding on her voyage. When the *Treveal* struck, the engines were put full speed astern.

(He could give no explanation as to how the *Treveal* got so near land; such things simply happened. (Press Interview))

He said he heard Captain Paynter direct the wireless operator to send out a most urgent message, and half an hour afterwards a message was received from the Admiralty that a tug was being sent between midnight and 1 a.m. Shortly after midnight the head wireless operator told witness that a general message had been sent out: 'For God's sake send assistance.' The ship was then full of water and witness had given up all hope of pumping it out. He had concentrated on keeping the dynamo going, and this he had done, enabling the ship's lights to be kept burning all night to attract attention. About 7 o'clock in the morning the vessel split along the side about 15 feet from the engine room floor, and he told the captain he would have to clear the men out of the engine-room, or they would be drowned. The tug was then visible, about two miles distant. The first explosive signal went up about 8 o'clock in the morning, and the tug was then at about the same distance. There was a very heavy sea running at the time. Witness was of the opinion that if the tug had come earlier she might have helped them. At about 8 o'clock the officers saw what they thought was smooth water inside Chapman's Pool, but it was dirty water from the clay washed down from the cliff, and they could not see the white caps of the breakers. They left the ship at about 9 o'clock. There was a small hut on the shore with a boat lying alongside it, which they thought would be a landing place, but they found the beach there was covered with rocks and boulders. They were making towards a pebbly beach when the boat was overturned, fore to stern, by a backwash wave from the cliff. He could not swim, but struggled towards the beach, and reached it, but was drawn back several times. He landed again on 'all fours, as weak as a rat,' and fell forward on his face, unable to move, although he could feel the water pulling him back. It was a clay bank, and he could not get any grip.

(The chief engineer said that men were struggling in the water in all directions ... Some of the men endeavoured to throw off their clothes, parts of which trailed in the water, proving a hindrance rather than a help. The scene at Chapman's Pool beggared description, with the piteous cries of the drowning men for succour that did not come. (Press Interview))

Witness saw no one on the beach except an able seaman named Winterbottom. Witness described how the two of them crawled up a gully without assistance, and eventually reached some old coastguard cottages. These, he understood, were only let for the summer, except that there was a Mr Gilderdale in one of them. Witness did not see any coastguards until 2 or 2.30 in the afternoon, when one or two came into the cottage and asked if they were the survivors of the *Treveal*.

Examined by Mr Cunliffe: (A letter was produced which Mr Thirkell had written to the owners after the disaster, stating,: 'I cannot express myself too strongly on the gross neglect of the responsible authorities, who drowned 36 men, as we had 12 hours' communication with them before the end.') Asked what, in his opinion, he thought the coastguards might have done, witness said that as the coastguards at St Alban's Head had themselves suggested Chapman's Pool for a landing, and knowing the coast and what the wind was, they should have roused the whole village and got assistance down on to the beach. There was no assistance of any kind. Witness explained that he did not see the Reverend Piercy and Mr Lander when he got ashore. He was on the beach 10 minutes, and took half an hour getting to the cottage, and in that time he saw no one. Asked what assistance he thought could have been given had there been people on the beach, witness replied that lines might have been thrown to the men in the water, and chains of men could have held hands. He had seen it done in worse circumstances - he had even seen chains of women out. Asked what, in his opinion, the tug might have done, witness said he thought that if the tug had brought a lifeboat, the lifeboat could have got under their lee and taken them off. There was 22 or 23 feet depth of water there. He did not suggest that in such weather the tug itself could have come alongside.

Examined by Mr Wilkinson: Witness said he was personally convinced of the danger during the night, and the men were very much upset, asking when the lifeboat was coming. He thought lines or chains of hands would have saved lives because a number of the drowning men touched the beach and went out again. He had seen lifeboats standing by all night when a ship was on a ledge or rock. He had seen coastguards standing by. Having, as he understood it, informed them that there was a landing at Chapman's Pool he thought some of them at least ought to have been on the beach during the night with a flare to guide them.

Mr Wilkinson: There was no reason why the coastguards should anticipate your leaving the ship.

Witness: They should anticipate danger at all times.

Re-examined by Mr Pilcher, with regard to the urgent message he said had been sent out soon after midnight, witness replied he was rather puzzled why it had not been received.

Mr Pilcher: Was it the following: '12.05 - *Treveal* to all ships: *Treveal* wants assistance immediately'?

Witness said he was given to understand it was more urgent than that.

Mr Pilcher said Mr Wilkinson had just handed him the copy of another message he was not aware of before: '12.14 - *Treveal*: Water two feet from dynamo. SOS.'

Witness said that would be the one.

By the Court: Witness did not see Third Officer Donald until he got to the cottage. While crawling up the face of the cliff he came upon another of the crew, a steward, who was pretty well gone.

(The Court adjourned.)

I was sitting in Captain Kemp's comfortable front room again. The old captain, hospitable as always, had served up tea and cake.

'I have a couple of photographs to show you,' I said and handed him the portrait of Captain Paynter. 'Do you know who that is?'

He looked at it long and hard.

'Is that Charlie Paynter?'

'Yes.'

'Well, he's a totally different man than I thought to see.'

'In what way?'

'Well, he's a nice, clean-looking man, isn't he.'

'He looks a very reliable man to me.'

'I never knew him personally, but they gave him a good name in St Ives when I was a boy, until the *Treveal* ... Can I pour you another cup of tea, or would you like a drop of something stronger? I can't offer you much I'm afraid -'

'Tea's fine ... Did Charlie Paynter like a drop of anything stronger, do you know?'

'No, I don't think he did. His people weren't drinking people anyway. His family was very well known in St Ives.'

'This is Third Officer Donald,' I said and handed him the photograph.

'He looks a brassy-looking bloke, doesn't he; as much to say, "I know what I'm doing." He knew what he was doing when he was on the bridge of the *Treveal*, didn't he.'

'I wanted to ask you about that Captain Kemp - about what you said about hearing that there was an uncertificated officer on the bridge.'

I showed Captain Kemp Donald's certificates and told him I didn't understand exactly when Donald would have become 'certificated'. Captain Kemp suggested that in this situation, when Donald did get his ticket, it would be 'backdated' in the ship's articles; it wouldn't be uncommon for that to happen. The captain would do it.

'So, Donald was a bona fide certificated officer in the *Treveal*?'

'Yes.'

'Did you ever meet him afterwards? He was a survivor, and he stayed on with the Hain line.'

I showed Captain Kemp the names of the ships Donald had sailed in after the *Treveal*. Captain Kemp looked down the list and then had another good look at the photograph.

'No, I never met him,' he said, finally.

I was disappointed, and put my next question to him with little hope of a positive answer.

'Thirkell, did you ever hear anything about him - the chief engineer, Robert Thirkell?'

I had barely finished the question before the reply came:

'He was saved. He was chief engineer in a ship I was in after.'

'Was he really?'

'Yes, one of Hains's ships.'

'What sort of man was Thirkell? What did you think of him?'

Captain Kemp laughed: 'Well, he was an engineer. I was never too friendly with engineers.'

'Are they a funny breed?'

'Well, water and oil never mix, you know.'

'Thirkell seemed to be very much Paynter's man -'

'Well, as a rule, chief engineer and a master at sea were more or less - if they were pally they would more or less go ashore together, and they really rely on one another in various jobs.'

'Was Thirkell married?'

'I don't think he was.'

'I think he was a Freemason,' I said.

'Yes, he would be just the type of man,' laughed Captain Kemp.

'Do you remember anything else in particular about Thirkell?'

'No, I don't think so.'

Chapter 4

I had extended my St Ives visit more than once, but the time was fast approaching when I would have to return home to Dorset. Much of my time had been spent on the trail of the leading figures aboard the *Treveal*, but what of the rest of the men? I had been unable to trace any official crew list, but had pieced together what I could from the Hain ledgers in the St Ives Museum, the death certificates of those who drowned and whose bodies were recovered, and the various lists which appeared in the contemporary press:

OFFICERS
Charles Paynter, 42, captain, St Ives.
Edwin H Hutchinson, 43, chief officer, Weston-super-Mare.
Charles C Tait, 22, second officer, West Hartlepool.
William J Donald, 21, third officer, Swansea.
   BOATSWAIN
E Phillips, Penzance.
   SAILORS
James E Bassett, St Ives.
William Bryant, 26, Mousehole.
A Kewn, Penzance.
Thomas Noall, 37, St Ives.
Henry Pearce, 57, St Ives.
W Richards, Penzance.
Arthur W Winterbottom, 19, Penzance.
   APPRENTICES
Frederick H Argall, 17, Truro.
Harold E Chumbley, 16, Stourport.
Kenneth Kirby, 16, Sheffield.
Douglas O Nidd, 16, London.
   COOKS &c
Allan Woolcock, cook, St Ives.
William U Phillips, 23, assistant cook, St Ives.
Thomas R Curnow, messroom steward, St Ives.
W A Symons, steward, Penzance.
Garfield Andrews, 19, assistant steward, St Ives.
   CARPENTER
Peter Cogar, 45, St Ives.

WIRELESS OPERATORS
Shaw.
Joseph Kavanagh, 21.
ENGINEERS
Robert H W Thirkell, chief engineer, Cardiff.
William B Whyte, 27, second engineer, Glasgow.
Harold Dobinson, 26, third engineer, South Shields.
W R Griffiths, fourth engineer, Barry.
OTHERS
'a Tynesider', name unknown; H Currie, 28, fireman; S Devlin, 24, fireman; Martin Donlon, 27, fireman; Patrick Foley, 30, greaser; Gallagher; C Gallon, 38, fireman; Peter Hendry, 46, donkey engine man; John Hosie, 35, fireman; McCotch or McCotneh; John McCallum, 32, fireman; McVeagh or McVeigh; Regan or Regas; J Rodden, 26, fireman; Peter Rooney, 27.

A glance at the list gives an indication of the extent to which the Hain company relied on local labour. It will be observed that the following were Cornishmen: captain, boatswain, seven sailors, one of the four apprentices, the ship's carpenter, and the cooks and stewards. The great majority of non-Cornishmen - the engineers and the 15 'others' listed - are confined to the bowels of the ship. Here are found Scottish and Irish surnames, an anonymous Tynesider, and the job description 'fireman' - those men, with 'small, fierce, resentful eyes', celebrated in Eugene O'Neill's 1922 play *The Hairy Ape*.

None of the 16 Cornishmen aboard the *Treveal* found themselves working in the most oppressive jobs aboard ship, and none of them disappeared into obscurity after the disaster. West County newspapers gave extensive coverage to a story which involved Cornwall's best known shipping company and which touched, directly or indirectly, so many families in the region. No Cornishman who survived the disaster arrived home unobserved or uncongratulated on his miraculous escape; no Cornishman who drowned went unmourned.

Five of the crew came from Penzance. The boatswain, Phillips, of Gothic House, Adelaide Street, and the steward, Symons, of 32 Rosevean Road, were both married men. The other three Penzance men were sailors and unmarried. Richards and Kewn were near neighbours of Symons: Richards lived at 15 Rosevean Road, with his father, a mason; Kewn lived with his mother at Rosevean Cottage, and would become 'the third son Mrs. Kewn has lost within about six months' (*Western*

Echo, 17 January 1920). Arthur Winterbottom, of New Street, who had served in the Navy during the First World War, would be the only Penzance survivor of the *Treveal* disaster.

Aside from William Bryant, a sailor, who came from Mousehole, just down the coast from Penzance, and Frederick Argall, the apprentice from Truro, whose brother I hoped to be speaking to soon, the other Cornishmen in the *Treveal* all hailed from St Ives.

Thomas Noall, like the Penzance sailor Winterbottom, had served in the Navy during the war. He was married, with three young children, and lived at 3 Court Cocking, a tiny nook of a street hard by the harbour.

Henry Pearce, of North Place, was an old St Ives sailor, with a wife in Liverpool: 'He was an uncle of the late Harvey Pearce, a brave young soldier whose coffined remains were sent home from an Edinburgh hospital, just twelve months ago where he died after being cruelly ill-treated and literally starved to death by the Germans, the military doctors describing the case as the worst they had seen' (*St Ives Times*, 16 January 1920).

James Bassett, 'sailor, unmarried, sole support of mother ... [was] the son of Mrs. Bassett, of 4, Bellair Terrace and nephew of Mr. William Blight, J.P.' (*St Ives Times*, 16 January 1920). His mother, Eliza Annie, was, according to a letter I had received from Mrs M Quick of St Ives, 'a woman who dressed very smartly.' James was 'a boy with a very attractive disposition. He was a Sidesman and Server at the Parish Church and was esteemed very highly by the Vicar and his co-church workers. He started life as an apprentice in the Printing Department of Mr. Martin Cock, where he again won the highest respect for his integrity' (*St Ives Times*, 16 January 1920). There was an ulterior motive for him joining the Hain company: 'James, it seems, was rather sickly and his mother hoped that a career at sea would improve his health' (Mrs Quick).

If Mrs Bassett had any concerns about the dangers her boy might encounter as a sailor, she may have found some comfort in looking at one of her neighbours in Bellair Terrace - Allan Woolcock, chief cook aboard the *Treveal*, who had been at sea 38 years, and 'had never been shipwrecked' (*St Ives Times*, 16 January 1920).

Woolcock's assistant in the galley was William Phillips, a young man who had recently suffered 'the horrors of being a prisoner of war in Germany'. The son of Mr and Mrs Ben Phillips, of Ayr Villa, he was a member of the Salvation Army, unmarried, and 'of a very cheerful disposition' (*St Ives Times*, 16 January 1920).

The stewards in the *Treveal* were Thomas Curnow, of Dove Street (messroom steward), Garfield Andrews, of the Wharf (assistant steward) - 'It was his first voyage with the firm, he having previously been at sea in a coasting steamer' (*St Ives Times*, 16 January 1920) - and the aforementioned Penzance man, Symons.

Finally, the ship's carpenter was Peter Cogar: 'married ... wife and 4 girls ... eldest son of the late Mr. Peter Cogar of [Quay Street] St. Ives, and prior to joining the Treveal was in the army for $3^1/2$ years, erecting huts in France' (*St Ives Times*, 16 January 1920).

Cogar's background is worth a closer look, for the circumstances of his appointment as ship's carpenter illustrate the nepotism which was endemic in the Hain company. Philip Thomas, of Saltash, had kindly responded to my letter in the *St Ives Times* (requesting information on the crew of the *Treveal*) with a family tree, showing his connection to Peter Cogar, and a wealth of information on the family. Mr Thomas wrote:

> Peter Cogar was born in St. Ives in 1876, the son of Peter & Betsy Cogar. Although a carpenter by trade, he came from a fishing background, the family owning a number of boats ...
>
> We don't know much about Peter Cogar's early life, except that before the 1st world war he spent some time in the USA (a brother had previously emigrated). During the war he spent some time in France.
>
> How he came to meet his wife we do not know but they married at St. Keverne on the 9th April 1903.
>
> Mary ('Minnie') Matthews came from Porthoustock on the Lizard peninsula where her family kept a small grocery & confectionary business ... She too came from a seafaring background, both grandfathers were coastguards and her father spent time in the Royal Navy ...
>
> Peter and Minnie lived in the family home at Porthoustock and with the dreaded Manacles reef just off shore, the family would have been only too aware of the destructive power of wind and sea. Surprisingly, given Peter's family sea-going connections there is no record of him going to sea until he contacted his cousin, William, in Sept 1919 ...

That cousin was William Cogar, Secretary of the Hain Steamship Company. William replied as follows:

Dear Peter,

In reply to your letter Capt F. Uren's address is Westbourne Road, Penarth. For your guidance however he has been seriously ill lately and will not return to business for about two or three weeks.

You do not state any reason for your enquiry. Are you thinking of going to sea?

I trust all your family are well and I was glad to hear you came through the campaign all right.

Yours sincerely,

William Cogar.

Peter wrote again and a further letter followed from William:

Dear Peter,

I have your letter and have written Cardiff asking to enter your name for a Carpenters berth as soon as possible. Berths are tightly held but I hope Mr Hughes will be able to do something for you. You should have some written evidence in your possession that you are a bona fide Carpenter as you have not been at sea as such before and the Board of Trade and Union are very particular. You will have to join the Union I expect.

The wages are £14 per month plus £3 per month as War Bonus which will probably continue for another six months.

Yours truly,

William Cogar.

The result of the correspondence which passed between them was that Peter Cogar was given the carpenter's berth in the spanking new ship SS *Treveal*. He and her master, Captain Paynter, were contemporaries: when they were children, both their families had worshipped in the Zion chapel. In Barnoon cemetery, I would discover on a later visit to St Ives, their memorial stones stand just a few feet apart.

The Inquiry
Second Day - Thursday, 6 May 1920 - Morning
ALLAN WOOLCOCK (Cook of the *Treveal*), examined by Mr Pilcher, said he was below in his berth when the *Treveal* struck on 9 January. He went on deck and saw St Alban's Head on the starboard bow. During

the night he observed Morse signalling between the ship and St Alban's Head. He first saw the tug *Pilot* in the grey of morning, about a mile and a half or two miles away on the starboard beam. He did not notice any Morse signalling on the tug. At 8 o'clock a heavy sea was washing over the *Treveal*, and the wind was increasing in velocity. Rocket signals were sent up at that time. The weather was a kind of wet haze. St Alban's Head could be seen through the mist. Soundings were taken, and there was 23 feet of water amidships on the port side. The *Treveal* was straining throughout the night and making noises showing that she was being damaged. Towards morning the noise became very loud. When they abandoned ship they got away from her very comfortably, the ship making a breakwater for them. Witness was one of 22 men in the captain's boat, all of whom were equipped with lifebelts. They made for Chapman's Pool. The sea that capsized the boat came from the starboard quarter. The captain had altered course. When witness came to the surface after the boat capsized, he saw the boat 20 yards away. There were five or six men on top. Witness could swim and he swam ashore. ('When the boat capsized I could not see much hope. There were some of us clinging to the boat, and I saw it was settling to the westward. I said "That's no good for me" and made for the shore.' (Press Interview))

Witness said he was helped ashore by the Reverend Piercy and Mr Lander. He was in the water about 20 minutes.

(Woolcock said that the seas broke so rapidly one after another, knocking the poor fellows under so often that there was no chance of a breather. After a severe buffeting about he was pulled out by the Reverend Piercy and Mr Lander, and collapsed just after, not remembering anything of the carrying up the cliff ... 'I believe I should have drowned if it had not been for the clergyman and the fisherman. I had the greatest difficulty in getting my feet.' (Press Interview))

Witness said the crew became anxious to leave the ship about midnight. He did not think it would have been safe to have left the ship at that time in the darkness, not knowing the place. He thought the time they did leave was the earliest time they could have left safely. If they had a guiding light ashore they might have left the ship earlier and have got ashore without casualty.

Examined by Mr Cunliffe: He thought the boat was 50 or 60 yards from where it could have been beached when it overturned.

Mr Cunliffe: If here had been people on the beach in the first place with a line do you think you would have experienced much difficulty in getting ashore?

Witness: No, sir.

Mr Cunliffe: If there had been people on the beach without a line do you think they could have helped you?

Witness: Yes. They could have formed a chain with their hands.

By the Court: There were other men near him struggling in the water and he had no doubt they could have been saved had a line been thrown from the shore. An ordinary heaving line would have sufficed. When he reached the beach he saw no one there. The Reverend Piercy and Mr Lander were running down the cliff at the time.

By Mr Cunliffe: The *Treveal*'s navigation lights were burning throughout the night. He was not sure about the cargo cluster lights.

ARTHUR WINTERBOTTOM (Able Seaman of the *Treveal*), examined by Mr Pilcher, said he went on watch at 8 p.m., after the *Treveal* left Portland on 9 January. There was a misty wind from WSW. He saw lights at Portland astern. He did not see the shore before the vessel struck. He saw a Morse signal from St Alban's Head and a reply sent from the ship during the night. The weather became worse in the morning. Now and again he could see St Alban's Head. He saw the tug about a mile and a half away. He did not hear the ship breaking up till after daylight. About half a dozen rockets were sent up. He left the *Treveal* in the captain's boat. About 70 yards from the shore the boat was capsized by a wave which struck it from port to starboard. He got ashore unaided.

(Winterbottom said that when the boat capsized he had to 'swim for it', and was in the water about a quarter of an hour. He reached the shore about the same time as Mr Thirkell, and, although in a very exhausted condition, was able to make for the cottage, where they received every possible succour. 'I consider I owe my life to leaving the overturned boat and swimming for land against the tide. I saw that we were drifting to westwards against the rocks and the cliff, where we should have no chance to land. I saw one of the crew washed against the rocks and try to get a hold but failed. Many of the crew were drowned through getting in this position. Nearly all the men had on lifebelts.' (Press Interview))

Witness said he did not see any villagers until he reached the cottage.

Examined by Mr Cunliffe: The Reverend Piercy and Mr Lander had not arrived when he got ashore.

Mr Cunliffe: When did you consider, if at all, that the lives of the crew were in danger?

Witness: I did not think they were in danger at all. I thought the lifeboat would come to us.

Mr Cunliffe: Were the men nervous at all?

Witness: No, they were all right.

Mr Cunliffe: If there had been volunteers on the beach do you think more lives would have been saved?

Witness: Yes, sir.

Mr Cunliffe: Give your reasons.

Witness: If they had lines every man would have been saved.

Mr Cunliffe: And if they had no lines?

Witness: I think a great number would still have been saved.

By the Court: He was of opinion that the tug *Pilot* could have towed a lifeboat into such a position that it could have saved the crew.

Examined by Mr Wilkinson: witness gave evidence in regard to the cargo cluster lights shown by the *Treveal* during the night.

ROBERT THIRKELL (Chief Engineer of the *Treveal*) recalled, said some of the lights should have been seen by a ship astern, or even to a point off the beam. They were very powerful lights.

(The other three crewmen of the *Treveal* who survived (the apprentices Argall and Kirby, and the mess steward Curnow) are not reported to have given evidence at the inquiry. Curnow and Kirby did not give interviews to the press in the immediate aftermath of the disaster either, probably because they were still suffering from the ordeal: Curnow, Chief Engineer Thirkell described as having been 'pretty well gone', while Kirby was the last life saved. Apprentice Frederick Argall, however, gave the following interview to the press, which completes the documented testimony of the *Treveal* survivors:

After the ship struck and the captain decided to abandon her, two boats were launched, and both tried to make the beach a mile away. When about 50 yards from the shore they both capsized. 'I had a miraculous escape,' he added. 'Men were struggling in the water all around me. Some clung to the upturned boats in the hope of holding on until assistance arrived. I swam a short distance but remembered nothing after I sighted the beach. I don't know how I got there, and that I was saved was nothing short of a miracle. I must have been washed in by the tide, and it was lucky for me that I was washed in the direction of the beach instead of the rocks, as several poor fellows were badly mutilated through being dashed against the rocks. I was told it was nearly an hour after I was picked up before I recovered consciousness.' He added that when they took to their boats they did not think they were in for such a rough time, believing that they would be able to reach the shore with a little effort.)

My visit to St Ives was over. On the morning of my departure I was standing on the 'Malakoff', a little man-made promontory with a wonderful view of the harbour and town to one side and the railway station and Porthminster Beach to the other. When the dead of the *Treveal* were returned to St Ives, crowds of people had lined the Malakoff and the Terrace above the railway station, as well as the station itself ...

On the morning of my departure, I had again telephoned Malcolm Donald, again without success, but had managed to conduct an interview over the telephone with Charles Argall, concerning his brother Frederick, the *Treveal* apprentice. Charles recalled his brother telling him about the lifeboats capsizing in Chapman's Pool: 'Fred said to me he remembered as boys I used to threaten him with a punch on the nose if he didn't dive off the quay in Cornwall. He said "when I realised I had to swim for it, I remembered your instructions. I kicked off my sea boots and dived off the lifeboat, and struck out for the shore."'

As I stood on the Malakoff and looked down on the railway station, I recalled an old black and white photograph, which Mrs Beach, Captain Paynter's great niece, had shown me, depicting the railway station in the early years of the twentieth century. As I stared at some indeterminate point in the middle distance, the old photograph displaced the modern vista.

Through the summer of 1919 steam trains pulled out of St Ives railway station, as they had for 50 years past: they crawled around the ledge cut in the cliff above Porthminster Beach, before disappearing into a tunnel half a mile away. Above and beyond the tunnel lay Treloyhan Manor, seat of the lately deceased Sir Edward Hain; and among the passengers aboard the trains were Hain company men - fathers, brothers, sons and husbands, who would be signing on in a Hain ship at some distant port; the last kiss of a loved one already just a memory.

In the town, along the Wharf, as the harbour filled and emptied under the summer sun, and in the shops in bustling Fore Street, or, on Sundays, outside the town's several churches and many little chapels - indeed, at all the places where groups of women happened to gather - the same chatter, with variant details, could be heard:

'My boy sails in the *Trevessa*, today.'

'I have a man in the *Tregurno*.'

'My father returns in the *Trevanion*, tomorrow.'

During the long years of the First World War the women had

endured shipping report blackouts. But those days were over: the newspapers were publishing the reports again, and any mother, sister, daughter, wife or sweetheart with a loved one in the *Treveal* would be able to follow the ship's progress halfway around the world, as the summer of 1919 drifted to autumn, and autumn gave way to winter:

Left Govan - Cardiff.	9 September.
Arrived Cardiff.	11 September.
Past Gibraltar - Port Said.	14 October.
Arrived Port Said.	23 October.
Left Suez - Calcutta.	3 November.
Past Perim - Calcutta.	6 November.
Arrived Calcutta.	20 November.

Of the outward leg of the *Treveal*'s voyage, little is known beyond the bare facts. She carried bunker coal from Cardiff to Port Said, and proceeded in ballast to Calcutta. The general atmosphere aboard the ship can readily be imagined. It was a cruel irony that for the crew of the *Treveal* it was the first in many a long year when putting to sea was not accompanied by lurking feelings of dread; indeed, for some of the men it was their first voyage since the end of the war. The war had claimed the life of Edward Hain (V) and precipitated the death of his father, and it had been a dark time for sailors. Mr H J Groves, who presided over the inquiry into the loss of the *Treveal*, noted particularly that the crew were, 'men who all through the war ... like the brave mercantile marine, of which we are all so proud, did their duty as heroes, running the gauntlet of a ruthless and unscrupulous enemy.' A feeling of entering a new and brighter era must have pervaded the crew and been reflected back at them by the shining steel of their new ship.

My interview with Charles Argall, on the morning of my departure from St Ives, had produced an account of an incident on the outward leg of the *Treveal*'s voyage, about which there was otherwise a dearth of information. It concerned the four apprentices. Frederick Argall was the only Cornish lad among them and although he was the eldest, by a couple of months, this did not apparently confer automatic seniority on him. Fred, his brother Charles recalled, although 'a hole-in-the-heart baby' was never one to duck a challenge: 'He was always good with his fists and I remember our father, who was a Methodist preacher, being shocked once when Fred was billed to fight the local Truro prize-fighter for a purse of £5.' The story in the Argall family is that Captain Paynter

Frederick Argall

addressed the apprentices at the start of the voyage:

'You've got to make up your minds, who is the senior of you four.'

Two of the apprentices were on the small side, and the captain turned to Fred and the other boy.

'You two had better fight it out,' he said.

The two boys did so and it was doubtless a popular result with the Cornishmen in the crew when the local lad Argall came out the victor.

What can be said about this incident? Was it a good spot of entertainment for a crew who during the long years of 'running the gauntlet' had little stomach for such diversions? - very probably. Was there an element of Captain Paynter engineering Cornish dominance among the apprentices, as in the wider crew? - perhaps. Was Captain Paynter a brutal man? - no, or certainly not by the standards of the day. Worse things could happen to boys at sea. James Hanley's 1931 novel *Boy* is a harrowing fictional account of the life of one unfortunate lad; while Captain Kemp's recollection of 'some hard men' in his early days with Hains, who included 'old Captain Gibson', who had locked up his apprentices for three days on bread and water, puts Captain Paynter's boxing match into perspective.

The *Treveal* arrived at Calcutta, the great port city of south-east India, on 20 November 1919. The crew went ashore, no doubt with the usual ebullience of sailors who have been cooped up for long periods. Old hands, who knew places a sailor could go for a good time in ports the world over, would have headed off for familiar haunts; those still wet behind the ears - such as Andrews, Bassett and the apprentices - would have tagged along with one group of shipmates or another. For some, who didn't know the ropes and who chose the wrong crowd, there might be rituals ahead, involving swearing, drinking, fighting and women, which could result in triumph or humiliation - and acceptance or rejection by the hardmen and bullies who are a part of any sizeable crew.

The *Treveal*'s principal cargo for the homeward voyage was jute, a plant whose fibres are used for making ropes, mats, bags and sacks. It was grown in the lowlands of the Ganges delta and was exported in vast quantities to Britain, where Dundee was the centre of manufacturing. However, like the *Treveal*, the jute trade was headed for disaster: 'The year 1919 was a good one for the Scottish jute trade. Dundee and its hinterland went into 1920 with yarn foresold as never before ... In 1920 the bubble burst ...' (S J Jones, ed: *Dundee and District*, p 172).

The *Treveal* was a doomed ship carrying a doomed cargo when she sailed out of Calcutta on 30 November 1919. The bulky and relatively light jute was offset by a quantity of manganese ore, so that her draught on leaving was, 'aft 24' 10", forward 25' 2"' (Report of Court), which appears to have been a satisfactory alignment for a ship of the *Treveal*'s size and design because no issue was raised in connection with it at the inquiry into her loss.

The Hugli River, on which Calcutta stands, and down which the *Treveal* sailed, is one of the mouths of the many-mouthed Ganges, and has an evil reputation among sailors. Its many perils are adequately described by some of the names they have been given: 'Mud Point'; 'James and Mary Sands'. Swift and dangerous currents and ever-shifting mud banks defy any captain of a ship to navigate the Hugli without a pilot. The Hugli pilots were an elite and picturesque body of men, with their own furniture and servants, and one of their number would have seen the *Treveal* headed safely out into the Bay of Bengal.

Thereafter, the *Treveal*'s route was the most economical for any steamship homeward bound from the East. She reported from Ceylon

(7 December), Perim Island at the southern end of the Red Sea (17 December), Suez (22 December), Port Said (Christmas Day) and Gibraltar (3 January). At Port Said, Captain Paynter signed on the 'Tynesider', no name recorded, and it was also at this time that he learnt that his first British port of call would be Portland, 'the vessel being instructed at the Suez Canal to call here' (*Southern Times*, 17 January 1920), in order to pick up a North Sea pilot.

Christmas and New Year having come and gone, the *Treveal* entered the western reaches of the English Channel. Countless ships, over the centuries, had made the same homeward approach. The swell which lifted the bow of the humble *Treveal* had also lifted the bows of the *Golden Hind*, the *Endeavour* and the *Victory*. The Channel provokes feelings in the hearts of English sailors which no other stretch of water can. It means home - a glimpse of the coast of Cornwall, actual or imagined; or at any rate the certainty of its proximity. For many of the men of the *Treveal*, of course - those who hailed from Cornwall - the day was all the more poignant. Homes, wives, sweethearts and families, for a time tantalisingly close, slipped away again; and in the late afternoon of Friday, 9 January, the Isle of Portland rose up off the port bow like, as Thomas Hardy describes it in *The Trumpet-Major*, 'a great crouching animal tethered to the mainland.'

Returning home from St Ives, I decided to call at Portland. It was evening when I drove out to the Bill, the southern tip of the Isle. I parked the car and surveyed the vast expanse of the English Channel. Natives of the Isle of Purbeck, like me, who are often derided by outsiders for insularity, are wont to look at Portland, that more geographically distinct peninsula at the other end of the county to our own, and say, 'Now, *there* is insularity.'

No place is more out-of-the-sea than Portland; no people more out-of-the-sea than Portlanders. This stretch of the Channel seems almost to be their own territorial water. Portland has bred its own for generations. It has its own laws, traditions and customs; its own minstrels of wind and wave. When Robert Brackenbury, landowning Methodist and friend of Charles Wesley, turned up to preach at Weymouth in 1791 he was 'promptly pointed to Portland where he was told "it is all darkness"' (Stuart Morris: *Portland*, p 42). The Islanders had a reputation for insolence and anarchy: the 'lerret', a boat unique to Portland, was admirably suited to the character of the people, having 'no sail, and the four or six oarsmen "... never keep stroke, but each side gets on as best it can"' (Morris, p 59).

At Portland Bill, in the gathering dusk, I gazed upon a group of men watching the embers of a driftwood fire, their fishing rods wedged in the rocks, waiting for a tug. In the gloom I imagined them as ghosts of others. One man shivered and clapped his hands behind his back. What's that? ... Foghorn? ... There it is again. A finger pointed at a looming shape on the sea that grew denser ... SS *Treveal*, an eye read through a spy glass. Tramp by the look of her, the other weather eye observed. India man? All nodded. Come a long way, though, she's sweating rusty red ... Fresh paint, though ... Look, she've got some pretty lines. All saw her change course. To pick up a pilot, I reckon ... I aint sid her before. Back to a huddle around the fire. Funny though, I wonder what she's after.

The harbour lay on the east side of this bare, almost treeless peninsula. Darkness was already closing in when the *Treveal* rounded the Bill and entered the quiet waters of Weymouth Bay. It was about 6 p.m. Across the bay, to the north, lights twinkled along the length of the Weymouth Esplanade. Between the great shoulders of Portland and the mainland, towards which the *Treveal* now moved, extended the enormous breakwater arms of Portland Harbour.

Portland Harbour

I started the car and drove round to where I could get a good view of the harbour. I parked behind the old convict prison. The prisoners had built it themselves; they had also built the breakwater - in the mid-1800s. The breakwater was a navigational hazard while it was under construction, a hazard compounded by 'the Trinity House pilots, three Portland brothers, whose fierce rivalry actually endangered the vessels they were meant to help!' - so much so that 'Most vessels managed to get by without their services' (Morris, p 76).

It was to pick up a pilot, not a local pilot, but a North Sea pilot, that Captain Paynter had called at Portland. As Captain Kemp at St Ives had explained it: 'I've taken ships all round, no pilots - I've been on the bridge five days coming up Channel and up to Dundee, and if you get too bloody tired you sit on a seat and have a man to wake you up - but that was just after World War One: there was a lot of mines laid in the North Sea that none of the masters knew anything about, so that's the reason Charlie Paynter wanted a North Sea pilot.'

When the *Treveal* came within signalling distance of the harbour, Captain Paynter gave the order to call up the Admiralty by Morse lamp, and to make the request that would bring the pilot boat swinging out into the bay to run alongside the *Treveal*: a quick step across dark water and the pilot would be aboard. Presently, the Admiralty replied. There was no North Sea pilot available, but letters would be sent out in an hour if the *Treveal* would care to wait. The *Treveal* did wait. She lay in Weymouth Bay, her engines being moved occasionally to hold her position. In the meantime Hains' Portland agents, Messrs Collins & Co, 'instructed Captain Paynter to proceed without [a pilot]' (*St Ives Times*, 16 January 1920) - ('That was often done' (Captain Kemp)) - and Captain Paynter wrote a letter to the owners, in which he stated that the *Treveal* had experienced 'a stormy voyage home' (*Western Morning News*, 12 January 1920). It does not appear that the *Treveal* was to proceed all the way to Dundee without a pilot, for it was reported in the *Western Echo* (17 January 1920) that 'the vessel left [Portland] ... for Dover'; at Dover, presumably, she would have picked up her pilot.

The letters which the *Treveal* was waiting for were brought out to her by the small steamer *St Keverne* and Captain Paynter's missive to the Hain company was handed down in return. At 7.43 p.m., immediately after the exchange of letters, the *Treveal* resumed her voyage at a speed of about nine knots.

An official in Lloyd's office at Weymouth, who watched her depart, laid a bet with a colleague that she would run aground.

Chapter 5

After all the hectic activity of my visit to St Ives, I was back on home soil.

For a good many years the village of Worth Matravers has been a haven for the comfortably off. Cottages have been carefully modernised, many are holiday homes and property prices are high. The air of tranquillity is such that on certain summer days the village appears to be uninhabited, or, rather, to be inhabited only by sightseers. While visitors from the nearby holiday resort of Swanage and ramblers who have taken a detour up from the coast path find the village, with its pub, church, tea room and pond, 'quaint' and 'unspoilt', its former inhabitants, if they rose up from their graves, would wonder if it was truly the place where they had lived, loved and died.

It takes some effort of imagination to stand in the heart of the village at the height of summer and to think back to a January day in 1920: to feel the chill of a bitter wind, to hear the clatter of a cart horse's hooves and to catch the stench of a score of drowned sailors. The pond then was not a mere backdrop for the eating of a pre-packed sandwich or the writing of a postcard. Known locally as Pond Head, it was muddy and weedy, and in spring would be choked with withies cut from the village willow trees, soaking, ready to make new lobster pots. The post office then sold a wide range of groceries and other goods, as well as stamps. The postmaster was Ralph Pushman, a dapper little man, who wore a brown suit, always with a tie, and shoes polished to a shine. On weekdays he wore a cap, which he carefully balanced with both hands in front of him, then threw up flat upon his head. On Sundays he wore a bowler hat. He was a Methodist, and lived by his Bible and by many maxims of his own composition, of which perhaps the chief was: 'A shopkeeper should be respectful but not servile.' The Methodist chapel, which stood next to the Square and Compass Inn, is today a private residence. The Reading Room of yester-year is now a tea shop. Only the inn, which took its name from the tools of the stone mason, retains its former function, preserved by Charlie Newman, great-grandson of the Charlie Newman who had it in 1920.

In the early decades of the twentieth century the road into Worth Matravers was a road to isolation - a ship's foghorn for a sea nymph siren and five white gates to be closed behind the traveller. The village was well removed from the old road through the Isle of Purbeck, from Corfe, via Kingston and Langton Matravers, to Swanage. One or two farmsteads only were in its immediate vicinity: to the west, Renscombe

Farm and Weston Farm; to the east, Eastington Farm, where the alarm had been raised when the *Halsewell* was wrecked in 1786, and where, in later years, the family would move on as room after room crumbled behind them. Parishioners still called their parson 'Daddy', 'Wold' Captain Reed lit the Reading Room fire and noisy seagulls scavenged in gardens.

Quarrying, fishing and farming were the principal industries in which Worth Matravers villagers worked. The first-named marked the landscape like a physical manifestation of the village's wariness of the outside world. Mounds of earth around the quarry shafts looked like defensive positions thrown up against an enemy, while tons of stone left outside to 'weather' through the winter seemed to have some obscure strategic purpose. There were no cringing poor where stone had to be wrested from the earth. Quarrymen and fishermen were fiercely independent - master and man together. Even the farm labourers at Worth Matravers had an independent streak. One, Amos Bower, christened 'A Mosquito' by a wit, was regularly sacked by his employer on Friday night - generally for insolence - only to turn up for work as usual on Monday morning. To other villagers of the Isle of Purbeck, Worth Matravers people were 'heathens', 'Wor' Bullies' and a law unto themselves.

Many of the villagers were staunchly liberal, an allegiance going back a hundred years to John Calcraft, of Rempstone Hall, owner of Worth Matravers and vast tracts of heath land. Calcraft had gained political notoriety when he defected from the opposition at the second reading of Lord Russell's Reform Bill (1831), enabling the bill to pass with a majority of one. Methodism was also strong in Worth Matravers. Their prayers were eminently simple - 'O Lord, teach us how to pray, and what to pray for' - and often brought the very tools of their workaday lives into the chapel: like an iron bar to a stone was sin addressed - 'O Lord, prise 'un out.'

The nearest the village got to the Establishment was the church, and the Church of England vicars; but at Worth Matravers many of those were eccentric, as if the barrenness of the landscape had stolen their reason. In the eighteenth century there was an incumbent, Samuel Marsh, who had 'the lamentable misfortune to go 'wicked mad' and to be confined in a floating lunatic asylum in Weymouth harbour ...' (E Caffery: *"A Church and a Chapitle, Wonderly wely bild."*, pp 24-5). In the late nineteenth century there was the Reverend Shepherd, who addressed a congregation of 'mongrel' worshippers, saying he would rather preach to six true Anglicans than a church full of Methodists. Much more had been said from that pulpit ... and much more was to come - from the Reverend Mearing, a strong Labour man, whose Christian Socialism finally got him removed from the parish, and from the Reverend Black, who preached against the gentry, of whom he said 'There are none in this parish - for that we should thank God.' No, the gentry were away from the place.

In September 1919, as the *Treveal* set out on her maiden voyage, Commander Guy Montagu Marston, RN, squire of Rempstone Hall, gave the village of Worth Matravers up for auction in lots. His former tenants, if they did not have the money themselves, begged, stole or borrowed it in order to bid for their own cottages. My grandfather, Frank Lander, had decided he could go to £100 but no more. Another villager, with either a powerful fancy for Frank's cottage or some harboured grudge, bid against him. The bidding rose to £100 with the other man having made the bid. Under the circumstances Frank may or may not have exceeded his pre-set limit of his own volition, but as it happened his daughter, Daisy, made the decision for him, elbowing him viciously in the ribs so that his arm went up in a reflex action. The bid won the day and Frank got to own his cottage.

Unlike some neighbouring villages, where the squire regulated every detail of his tenants' lives (no one but the shepherd was allowed to keep a dog, for example), in Worth Matravers the villagers had been largely left to get on with things in their own way. 'Captain' Marston had been a good landlord. He had rented cottages at just £5 a year and he was never seen or heard from, except at Christmas-tide when every tenant had delivered, by pony and trap, a round of best beef. A very old heath woman, when once asked what she thought of Commander Marston, replied, 'I think he will go to heaven all right - and Squire Calcraft.'

At the time, no villager saw that a whole culture had come to an end. Today, though, the two years which saw the end of the First World War, the selling of the village and the *Treveal* disaster stand as a watershed between how things were and the accelerated evolution of the village into what it has become.

From the 1920s onwards Worth Matravers began to be 'discovered' by an increasing number of people from affluent society, who appreciated an out-of-the-way place for weekend breaks and summer holidays. The artist Augustus John and the well-known barrister, and afterwards judge, Jellinek, became regular visitors, and a veritable stream of actors and their 'lady friends' put up at the Square and Compass Inn.

On summer days, between the Wars, when the sun rose big and round, visitors would flock to Chapman's Pool, canvas picnic bags hurriedly filled with sandwiches in strong, brown paper bags, cakes in large square biscuit tins and 'pop' in half-pint milk bottles tied down with greaseproof paper. Cresting Chapman's Pool Hill, the farthest point of distance seen would be the shimmering haze above Egmont Rocks on the west side. The Pool would have a kind of purple regality, smooth as silk. Green seaweed would swirl around in a slack tide, bubbly water would break along the shore with a slight hiss like champagne, and an hysterical dog (there always is one) would bark hoarsely and prance backwards on its hind legs, pleading for just one more stick to be thrown. When the fishermen came ashore in their boats, the visitors would run around the beach, hoping to buy fresh fish - 'Wrap them in this,' someone would say, holding out a wine-stained copy of *The Times*.

For Worth Matravers people, scraping a living from sea, soil or stone, visitors afforded an opportunity for making 'a bit extra'. At one end of the scale of enterprise, a boy could earn a penny for opening a gate; at the other end, one villager condescended to share his wife with a London actor. Whenever the man was down, the husband could be found wandering the village at all hours of the night. Asked 'What are you doing?', the reply was, 'Well, he do help pay the rent.'

At the time the *Treveal* went aground, the village of Worth Matravers had made the first small step towards its future, while its other foot remained gripped by the past. Elements of both would play their parts in the disaster.

The Inquiry
Second Day - Thursday, 6 May 1920 - Morning (continued)

HORACE PIERCY (Curate of Worth Matravers), examined by Mr Pilcher, stated that at about 9 a.m. on 10 January he heard the sound of what he thought was a gun and heard it again two minutes later. He met a fisherman called Lander and they went together towards Chapman's Pool. They looked to see if the flag was at the top of the flagstaff at the St Alban's Head coastguard station, which, with a rocket signal, he understood, was the signal for calling out the volunteer life-saving company. They saw no flag. On reaching a point where the Channel came into view, Lander saw the *Treveal* on Kimmeridge Ledge. The weather was very thick, with hard rain and wind. They stayed two or three minutes, debating whether to go back and get help or to go on, but concluded that the ship must have been seen from the coastguard station. They went on. On arriving at a point overlooking Chapman's Pool, they saw two boats floating bottom up, with certainly 20 men clinging to them, and others struggling in the water. The boats were about 50 yards from the shore. They were not actually in the surf. There was a line of surf across the entrance to the Pool, and heavy surf around the edge. Witness and Lander ran down to the beach. The chief engineer and another man (Winterbottom) had already managed to gain the shore, one of whom pointed to a man (Woolcock) who was being rolled over and over in the surf. Witness and Lander went into the surf and pulled him out. They then saw others struggling in the surf and witness went in and pulled the third officer out. Witness and Lander succeeded in pulling out three more men alive.

(The men were terribly exhausted, one (Argall) being unconscious. Witness and Lander helped to bring him round, getting a quart of water out of him ... Every man saved had on a lifebelt. (Inquest))

They also got the body of the chief officer ashore, at about 11 a.m., and tried artificial respiration for an hour without success. The survivors were taken off the beach. No coastguard came down to the beach while witness was there. It was not until midday that any coastguard was seen, and that was one from the next station. When he saw the upturned boats in Chapman's Pool it was between 9.30 and 9.45 a.m. The last man saved (Kirby) was brought ashore at 11.20 a.m. Witness said that after seeing that no more men could be saved he went to the St Alban's Head coastguard station. In witness's opinion the men struggling in the water were so close that lines thrown from the shore would have been of great assistance. A chain of men could not have reached more than 10 yards owing to the shelving beach. Witness himself was washed off his feet twice by the backwash.

Examined by Mr Cunliffe: The members of the volunteer life-saving company were mainly fishermen who were well acquainted with Chapman's Pool. About 30 fathoms of line held at the beach would have been of great benefit.

(Witness said if only a line had been sent over the boats he considered that a majority of the men clinging to the boats could have been saved. There was in the Pool an eddy in which the boats were caught and whirled about for some time. There would have been plenty of time for lines to have been got across. The last man to fall away from the boats did so quite three quarters of an hour after witness and Lander got there.

One of the men said that the only reason he left the upturned boat was because he did not see anyone on the beach. *The Coroner*: The jury, I expect, have their own opinions, and I would not like to add anything of hearsay. (Inquest))

Witness said he went to St Alban's Head coastguard station between 12.30 and 1 p.m. None of the coastguards had left then. They knew that the vessel was there but not that men had come ashore. Witness said that when he left the village that morning he did not know the ship was off Chapman's Pool and remarked to Lander that they might be going on a wild goose chase.

Mr Cunliffe: This is a public court and on behalf of the owners I wish to thank you and the gentleman associated with you for the very gallant way in which you behaved.

Witness: I only wish we could have done more.

Examined by Mr Wilkinson: He thought it possible that the sound of the rockets might have been heard in the village and not at St Alban's Head.

A Member of the Court: Do you think the coastguards at St Alban's Head could have seen the boats leave the *Treveal*?

Witness: Yes, if they had kept their eyes open.

(According to Nina Warner Hooke, who interviewed Mr Piercy many years later: '[He] said, "Yes, if they could have kept their eyes open". In his mind was the memory of fighting his way out towards the Head with Frank Lander and the difficulty of opening their eyes against the driving sleet. The reply was badly expressed ... and in the report of the proceedings it was given as: "Yes, if they had kept their eyes open."' ('Avoidable Loss' in *Dorset*, No 70, p 15))

Mr Warner: The court wish to express to you their appreciation of your action in saving these lives. I know what it means to be in a backwash and you must have risked your life in saving these men.

In the aftermath of the *Treveal* disaster a photograph of Horace Piercy and a short paragraph on his background adorned local and national newspapers. The *Bournemouth Daily Echo* (19 January 1920) had more to say. Under the heading 'HEROIC VICAR' the *Echo* began: 'The Rev. H. M. M. Piercy, the gallant clergyman who was instrumental in rescuing some of the crew from the wreck near Swanage last week-end, will be known to many Bournemouth people. He is a Bournemouth man, having lived here all his life till his marriage. He is the youngest son of Mr. and Mrs. G. J. Piercy, now residing at "Fernbrake," Canford Cliffs ...' The newspaper continued, recalling his 'SERVICES IN THE WAR' as 'one of four sons of whom Mr. and Mrs. G. J. Piercy have every reason to be proud.' Horace had 'a creditable record', serving in the Royal Army Medical Corps: 'As a Cambridge man, he declined the commission he could have had, and ere long was discharging duties on which his heart was set in German East Africa.' The report mentioned the naval career of another son, and detailed the several infirmities among other members of the 'GALLANT FAMILY', which prevented them, much to their disappointment, from entering the fray.

Horace Piercy

Horace Piercy had arrived in the village of Worth Matravers on a warm spring day in 1916, to take over from the lately deceased Reverend James Edwards, or 'Daddy Hong Kong' as he was known. On the morning of Mr Piercy's arrival Ralph Pushman, the village postmaster and grocer, had opened up for business as usual. The usual customers came and went. Mrs Amos Bower, as was her habit, came walking slowly towards the shop, her bag swinging to the rhythm of her measured step. Her clothes had seen better days on a winter's bed. She entered the shop, placed one hand across her commodious stomach, the other on the puffy, work-worn wrist of the first, and looked along the shelves. Mr Pushman waited. 'Now then,' she said, 'what shall us 'ave?' Her order eventually given and weighed out in careful ounces, she was done. Mr Pushman 'booked it'. He knew she had shaken her husband's 'pub clothes' in the hope of a coin falling out, and he also knew that no matter how long it took her she would pay off her bill.

As Mrs Bower left the shop, Mr Pushman followed her to the door, looked out and then returned to his paperwork: 'Fifteen at two shillings is one pound ten shillings. Ten at half a crown is one pound five shillings ... Chapel fire to be lit on Sunday; Mr Hubbard this week ... Several quarter dozen tins to be ordered from Locks ... My word, that ham smells good' - he suddenly looked up and listened - '... Car coming ... a noisy one ...' Mr Pushman got up and went to the door. It was not a car, but a motor cycle. A motor cycle with a strong-looking wicker sidecar, like a ship's fender. The rider stopped and removed his goggles, stood astride the machine, and looked around. Finally, he turned to Mr Pushman and asked, 'Have you any ginger beer?' (He pronounced it *bear*.) 'Yes, we have,' Mr Pushman said; and, hearing such a polished accent, produced - respectfully but not servilely - not only the bottle of drink but a glass to go with it.

Mr Piercy and his wife took up residence in the grand vicarage. At Pond Head, where the feature of village men lounging on the paving flags discussing matters affecting their lives was so common that it had been given a name - the Pond Head Parliament - the new arrivals were the talk of the day. Where the Reverend Edwards had been a timorous man, as thin as a hurdle, with a little white terrier, always trembling whatever the season, the Reverend Piercy had breezed into the village on his motor cycle like a breath of fresh air. He was a handsome and well-educated young man, who, it was said by his family (according to gossip), had married beneath him. Mrs Piercy made all her own clothes, played the church organ and was a devoted wife. One villager who knew her described her as a 'worthy' woman.

Although, in the opinion of his parishioners, the Reverend Piercy was no preacher, his enthusiasm for village activities and easy-going manner won him much popularity. The annual events of the calendar, such as the Rogation Day procession, were glorious festivals under his curacy. He had a great fondness for the young 'maids' of the village, whose simple, country innocence seemed to lift his soul; and he took groups of them on heady summer picnics. Of course, a number of the girls had minor crushes on him, so perhaps what was food for the soul was also food for the man.

News of the growing carnage of the First World War began to prey on Horace Piercy's mind, until the conviction welled in him that, for the time being at least, his duty lay elsewhere - and away he went, not as an officer and padre but as a private in the Royal Army Medical Corps. The call of God was less urgent than the cry of 'Stretcher-bearer! Stretcher-bearer!', although he was unable to respond to it ceaselessly: 'he was on two occasions taken seriously ill with malaria' (*Bournemouth Daily Echo*, 19 January 1920). That the idyllic days he had enjoyed at Worth Matravers were very much in his mind while he recuperated is sufficiently suggested by a postcard he sent to Daisy Lander, one of the young belles of the village: 'I am thinking of you at the service of Intercession.'

Horace Piercy returned from the First World War to his parish, where the church bells were rung to welcome him home. Two men rang the welcome. Ted Pushman, the postmaster's boy, being a Methodist, was quite restrained in his ringing, but Charlie Hooper's ringing was relentless, pulling the ropes as if to open the gates of Heaven, finally being brought back to his senses by the appearance of the curate, shouting his thanks for the welcome.

After the initial euphoria of his return it may have been that the parish seemed to Mr Piercy less idyllic than formerly. What had previously been merely the day-to-day features of its principal industry were now reminders of the horrors of a war which he doubtless wished to forget. All around him men tunnelled and sweated, and squeezed and squatted, and swore at blocks of stone; while the blasts of high explosives boomed from the more distant cliff quarries. Indeed, from an incident which occurred soon after his return, it appears that Mr Piercy felt he had come home to a godforsaken place.

The church at Worth Matravers has a traditional shape: chancel, nave and west tower. The walls are of local rubble, the stonework splattered with explosions of lichen. The interior is rather gloomy, the light struggling through the recessed stained-glass windows along the east and west walls. On spring days, when clouds race over the sun, the hue of the congregation constantly changes: one moment pews of shadows, the next bathed by sunlight. Such ambivalent colouring could throw a man from his purpose, but not the Reverend Piercy. He had experienced the deep blackness of war, which at least, whatever the weather, would allow him to say what he had to say. On the day in question he came down from the pulpit and stood in the chancel, on a level with his congregation, and with the voice of a man shocked out of his wits accused the whole village of immorality. It was the talk of the village for months afterwards. Many said the war had changed him. Others observed that the innocent maids of whom he had once been so fond had, in his absence, grown up and drifted in and out of relationships, as is the timeless tenor of village life. Whatever had prompted his bitter remarks, the village found it hard to forgive him.

The Inquiry
Second Day - Thursday, 6 May 1920 - Morning (continued)

FRANK LANDER (Fisherman of Worth Matravers), examined by Mr Pilcher, said he was a member of the volunteer life-saving company. Just after 8 o'clock on the morning of 10 January he heard rocket distress signals.

(He heard the first at 8.20 and the last at 9.05 a.m. (Inquest))

Thinking the volunteer company had been summoned he went out. He called for his neighbour but the man, who was a member of the volunteer company, refused to come out. Witness met Mr Piercy and they went together to Chapman's Pool. There were about 20 men on the upturned boats. On running down to the beach, witness passed the chief engineer and another survivor (Winterbottom). Witness and Mr Piercy pulled one man (Woolcock) out of the water, then clasped hands to pull out four more. They also pulled out the chief officer. The chief officer's head was badly injured and they could not revive him. Witness stated that the weather throughout the morning was very thick and there were intervals when he could not see the *Treveal*. There had not been much wind until 7 o'clock that morning, when it freshened. He first saw coastguards at Chapman's Pool at 2 o'clock and heard that they had been there two hours. It was witness's opinion that if they had a line more lives would have been saved. It would have been impossible to throw heaving lines as far as the boats, but with lines held ashore and a good swimmer to carry them out more lives might have been saved. Witness saw men on the upturned boats for three quarters of an hour. He estimated that the boats were 20 yards from the shore. The men were washed off the boats one by one. Witness stated that landing at

Chapman's Pool would have been safe at low or half tide, but that at high tide the place was a death trap. He did not think it possible for the *Treveal* to have been driven off Kimmeridge Ledge and thrown on St Alban's Head. No vessel once on the Ledge had come off again.
(The Court adjourned for lunch.)

Afternoon

FRANK LANDER (Fisherman of Worth Matravers), recalled, and examination by Mr Pilcher continued: Witness gave evidence relating to the volunteer life-saving company. The company, which numbered 13 men, was usually called out by signal from the coastguard station, and acted under orders of the chief officer at St Alban's Head. Mr Charlie Newman, at the Square and Compass Inn, was the captain of the volunteer company. The company was called out by a flag signal in daytime or a lamp at night, on the flagstaff at St Alban's Head. All the gear was kept at the Head. Some years ago there was a lifeboat at Chapman's Pool. It was under the charge of the chief boatman at a coastguard station at Hill Bottom, near Chapman's Pool. It would be very difficult to get the tackle and breeches buoy to Chapman's Pool. The gear was stowed in a horse cart, but no horse was kept for it. Witness was of opinion that if the whole gear had been at Chapman's Pool more lives - but not all - would have been saved. He thought that if the tug *Pilot* had brought a lifeboat in tow it could have come half or a quarter of a mile inside the *Treveal* in deep water. He could not say if the lifeboat would have been able to get to the wreck. It would have been dangerous work. Witness was of opinion that if the *Treveal*'s boats had entered Chapman's Pool farther east they would not have capsized. Had a man who knew the landing place been present he could have directed the boats and brought them safely ashore. The first coastguards to arrive were from Kimmeridge. Before that two men (Mont Hooper and Walter Welsh) and two women (nowhere are the two women named, although one was probably Mont Hooper's daughter, Floss, who was married to Walter Welsh) had arrived from Worth Matravers and assisted in the artificial respiration and carrying the survivors up to the old coastguard cottages.
Mr Cunliffe: I see what you did and what Mr Piercy did, but what did the coastguards do?
Witness: I don't know, sir.
Mr Cunliffe expressed the thanks of the owners to the witness for his gallantry.

By Mr Wilkinson: He thought that if the men had left the *Treveal* at daybreak, 7 a.m., it would have been low tide and quite safe.

The Court expressed its appreciation of the witness's gallant conduct and complimented him on the manner in which he had given his evidence.

JOHN DAINTREE (Senior Inspector of Life-Saving Apparatus to the Board of Trade), examined by Mr Pilcher, said he inspected St Alban's Head station in April last year. There was a full apparatus at St Alban's Head. On the occasion of his inspection the company did a good drill. The life-saving company should be 21, including coastguards. It was the duty of the company to work under the orders of a coastguard if one was present. Witness did not think a telephone from St Alban's to the village was necessary. The signal system had never failed. Asked if he thought the rocket apparatus would have been any use at Chapman's Pool, witness said the apparatus could not have been got down to the Pool in less than two hours, and that the ship was too far away for the rocket apparatus to have been used. If, however, the evidence was correct that the men were clinging to one of the upturned boats for three quarters of an hour, lifelines could have been fired over the boat. Witness was of the opinion that heaving lines could not be used at more than 15 yards on account of the danger to men on the boat.

Mr Wilkinson asked if the whole company should have been called out and the rocket apparatus got ready.

Witness: I consider the company ought to have been called out directly the coastguards were aware that the vessel was ashore, even though the ship had given no signal of distress and the full rocket apparatus would have been of no use at that time.

By the Court: The coastguards, even without the volunteers, could have taken down the lifelines and lifebuoys.

Frank Lander, his brothers and their families had lived all their lives in and around Worth Matravers. The first Landers had come rowing and sailing into the Isle of Purbeck from the Channel Islands in about 1630 and settled like hens over eggs. There is a pedigree of the Landers of Purbeck which shows them as people of some substance, leaving wills and estates, and holding positions such as ship's captains, Harbour Master of Poole, Mayor of Poole, and Collector of Customs. Thus, perhaps, it was some resonance of this past that encouraged the humble fisherman Frank Lander to have his 'Sunday best' suit made in London of navy blue pilot cloth. After a day's use his wife, Jane, used to brush it and put it away in a tin trunk at the top of the stairs, in the stone-built cottage Down the Lane. There the family lived: Frank, strong and quiet, who would have bled the sea if he had cut himself; Jane, thin, quick, superstitious, religious and wise; and their children, Sid, Dora and Daisy Kate.

Many times in my life, and in all seasons and weathers, I had walked the fishermen's route to Chapman's Pool. I walked it several more times in the months following my visit to St Ives, reacquainting myself with sights, sounds, smells and memories, the better to describe a day in my grandfather's life.

Frank Lander, master fisherman, closed his cottage door as noiselessly as he could and made his way up the cobbly lane. The summer night air was cool and the sky spangled with stars. Frank tapped at Miller Lander's door. Miller, a 'thirds' man, came out and the pair stumbled up Pike Lane to the main road, which went round with the vicarage wall. On they tramped for half a mile, past Renscombe farmhouse and its barns - silent except for munching cows - up a rising field to a stile;

Frank Lander

79

then over, and down a long path to the boat houses at Chapman's Pool, part of the sea border of Encombe Manor (anciently the home of Lord Chancellor Eldon), a well-kept estate, abutting the western boundary of the 'heathen' parish of Worth.

Without the gaiety of the visitors who would flock to it in the coming years, Chapman's Pool was a lonely, sombre, crumbling place, the black shale cliffs which enclosed it slowly falling, ton by ton, into the sea. In an ancient report dealing with the defences of England it was spoken of as a creek where two or three boats may land, but not dangerous for any great attempt of the enemy. Always there was the tinkle of cascading shale splinters; and, from time to time, in very hot weather, a cow leaning over the cliff's edge to feel the up-draught would take a step too far and plummet to the beach below - the carcass ending up as fishermen's bait.

There were people born at Worth Matravers who had never been to Chapman's Pool; it might have been Calcutta as far as they were concerned. Most children today are taught from an early age that water is a friend - to gambol and frolic in - but attitudes were once much different. The few villagers who did go to the Pool in the era of the *Treveal* - on the few summer days when it presented a beguilingly friendly face - kept their children out of the sea and a weather eye open for the freak wave that could dash in and sweep the unwary away. No local fisherman could swim a stroke. It was a proud boast; they had too much respect for the sea.

The Worth Matravers men who regularly fished out of Chapman's Pool were George and Mont Hooper in the *Dove*, Frank and Miller Lander in the *Fly*, and Andrew Squibb and partner in the *Sunbeam*. Their boats and huts huddled around the 'Dock' at the east side of the Pool. A huge concrete wall held back the land mass, and inside this wall there was a wooden construction - empty when it had not an Encombe Estate boat in it - called 'Government House'. Next door to Government House was a large, stone boathouse, where Edwin Bower kept his boat and all his gear. Edwin, who lived next door to Frank at Worth Matravers, was a mystery man. He kept himself to himself and fished (as and when the fancy took him) alone. No one ever asked or knew how he came to have such a fine boathouse. Beyond it was a capstan for pulling up the boats; and well back, facing due west, towards Portland, were the fishermen's huts.

Frank and Miller arrived at Chapman's Pool. The night had not yet departed, nor morning yet arrived. The white and black tarred boats -

14 feet long and about 5 feet wide - were barely visible, moored just off-shore. There were lobster pots for new ground already aboard the boats and buckets of stinking bait. Then it was the open sea - not enough breeze to get a sail up, so long, back-pulling strokes with the oars to where the first pot's cork should appear. Once over their fishing ground, marked by a tall, coastguard chimney, they rowed slowly around on a gentle swell, watching every ripple. Suddenly a cork popped up as if from the neck of a bottle and then began the long, slow haul, until the pot was pulled aboard, gushing with water, and revealing a huge, tail-whipping lobster ... or a spider crab, like a truncated ballerina ... or a common crab, with claws like a wrestler's shoulders ... or a bale of seaweed. The sun rose in the sky, seagulls came around and the bait stank to the height of the now starless heaven.

The day was bright and open, but before every dawn there lurked deep fears and superstitions. Who at sea would dare to drink out of a black bottle, or not be careful about what he did on a Friday? Deeply and broadly were these superstitions known. Frank Lander, when a mature man, had to have an operation in a London hospital. He was told the date ... a Friday. An emotion of concern must have crossed his face, for the surgeon said, 'You don't like the day, do you?' - and he changed it. As well as the superstitions, there were fears. In the lore of the Worth Matravers fishermen there were 'holes' in the sea-bed of the coastal waters they worked. What creatures might inhabit these holes? A puffing grampus, a gruff-voiced conger eel, Leviathan, orc, basking shark? After all, monsters did once swim in these seas. The great depth of water around St Alban's Head once furnished a strange tale, not solved to this day. The incident occurred when Frank and Miller were hauling pots off the Head sometime during the First World War. Pot corks had appeared, the water was slack and all was as normal. Suddenly they stopped what they were doing. What was that noise? Both had heard a deep, rumbling sound coming from the bottom of the sea. Louder and louder the sound grew, until, with a great roar, the surface of the water was broken - by the bow of a submarine. Frank and Miller rowed furiously away, for they had seen the insignia of the enemy. They reported the sighting, but were swiftly dealt with by a man from the Admiralty who *told* them that if it was a submarine at all, it was a British submarine. Frank's final opinion was that the lobster pots they were hauling had dragged over the submarine's hull, so that it surfaced to see what was going on. This was possible because the pots they made then were huge; big enough to catch an unwary grampus. When Frank had finished making a pot he often used to sit his wife on it. She weighed seven stones; if the pot didn't sag it was just about right.

The fishermen earned a meagre living. Crabs were sold at 4d/lb, lobsters at 8d/lb. The real breadwinner was the cooked bright red prawn. Dozens of crates were sent by rail from Swanage for the London Lord Mayor's Banquet every year. They were graded 2d for a regular mouth-watering prawn and $2^1/_2$d for a 'corker'. They were counted out in hundreds by the fishermen's wives and one put at the head of each pile. Fishermen's wives had not to be squeamish. They had to cook all the fish in a big boiler. Lobsters and prawns were dropped into boiling water; crabs into cold water and slowly brought to the boil. Sometimes a conger eel would be brought home, and bark and thump up and down in its box. Once or twice a week fishmonger Brown would come up from Swanage to take the shell fish and leave bait for the pots. The fishermen had an audit-proof way of paying themselves. The senior partner (master fisherman) kept two thirds of the income and was responsible for buying the gear and maintaining the boat. The other man received one third but had no expenses. In winter the fishermen's income was augmented by quarrying.

Much of my grandfather's experience of life had to do with the sea; of the dangers of a sudden squall, a freak thunderstorm, or the breaking of white water in a fog. Most of the stories he told are now forgotten, although his wife, Jane, who outlived him by many years, used to say that any yarn he began she could always finish. The one or two of his sayings that we remember were practical observations which related to his two occupations: that the month of August is all gust, and that on 12 January you can see to work a stone outside with a mason's tools.

It need hardly be said that in the aftermath of the *Treveal* disaster no photograph of Frank Lander graced the newspapers and no tribute to *his* family was penned.

Chapter 6

Thomas Hardy writes in *The Dynasts* of two men with pikes looming up on duty as beacon-keepers beside the ricks. Hardy stirs them into argument about which way they should be facing. One says 'Black'on is the point we've to watch, and not Kingsbere; and I'll tell 'ee for why ...' The other beacon-keeper says, nevertheless, he is going to keep an eye on Kingsbere, 'because that's more likely o' the two ...' Can orders ever be plain enough?

It might be said that the old beacon-keepers were the vanguard of the modern coastguard service. The old keepers were watching against an enemy - the French. The new coastguards were almost swamped with duties:

> In 1809, the Government established a Preventative Water Guard to operate in coastal waters, to tackle any smugglers who had managed to evade the Revenue cruisers further out to sea and to check on the effective functioning of the Revenue cruisers themselves. It was also responsible for giving assistance when a ship was wrecked...
>
> In 1856, after the Crimean War - during which the Coastguard first functioned as a reserve force for the Royal Navy - control was transferred to the Admiralty. During the next 70 years, the service acquired a variety of different responsibilities, ranging from those laid down in the Coastguard Service Act 1856 (to provide for the defence of the coasts of the realm, the more ready manning of the Royal Navy in the event of war or emergency, and the protection of the revenue), to assisting vessels in distress, taking charge of wrecks, operating life-saving apparatus, participating in the lifeboat service, searching for mines and torpedoes lost at sea, and performing sundry duties in connection with signals, telegraphs, buoys, lighthouses, wild birds and rare fish washed ashore.
>
> (Public Record Office: 'Records of H M Coastguards')

Had these men beds to go to? This list of a coastguard's many duties is perhaps reflected in a description of an over-dressed, over-loaded Victorian 'watcher':

> As the speaker moved forward into the moonlight, I at once

recognised an old acquaintance, one of the coast-guardmen. The latter fact was sufficiently proclaimed by the heavy cutlass hanging at his side, as well as the butts of a pair of enormous horse pistols protruding from the broad belt that encircled his rotund waist. A tarpaulin hat with a long flap, commonly called a "sou'-wester," contained a round, bullet-shaped head, covered on the upper surface with curly, pepper-and-salt coloured hair, and on the under, ditto with ditto. An oilskin coat, thrown widely open, hung over his shoulders and back, and oilskin continuations encased his nether man; under one arm was a telescope, the coast-guardman's inseparable companion ... ('The Coast-Guardman's Yarn' in *Boy's Own Paper*, No 26, Vol I, 12 July 1879, p 413)

One wonders how often he saw a grampus 'blow' or a bright blue paddy bird. How was all his activity co-ordinated, and by whom, and from where?

In the early days of the service, coastguards were more active, routinely patrolling the cliff paths. On the Purbeck coast, as elsewhere, each station regularly contacted its next door neighbour. The path they used was often dangerously near the edge of the cliff and it was marked for safety by a line of heavy stones, kept freshly whitewashed, as a guide in foggy weather and to reflect the lights of lanterns carried by men on night patrol. Even so accidents happened: one Thomas Lavery, buried in Kimmeridge churchyard, died after 'accidentally falling over the cliff in the execution of his duty' on an October night in 1839.

L G M Bond, in her book *Tyneham,* writing about the coastguard service at Worbarrow, recalled an incident in which two men were thrown out of a boat by a sudden squall (p 58): 'The Worbarrow chief officer of coastguard was away and his second in command refused to shoulder the responsibility of taking out the lifeboat without orders. While he was telephoning to headquarters for instructions ...' the men were saved by the prompt action of the coastguards' wives who launched the boat themselves. Perhaps a reason why some would-be life-savers wait around - refuse 'to shoulder the responsibility' - is simply because in the past the coastguard service has been administered by so many different departments and the parameters of responsibility have changed so much.

At the time the *Treveal* went aground the nearest coastguard stations were at Kimmeridge and St Alban's Head. As recently as 1910 there had been men stationed at Hill Bottom, the valley which drops into Chapman's Pool, but the four cottages had been sold off and were holiday homes, occupied only for a few summer months each year. There had also been at Chapman's Pool, in years gone by, a lifeboat. The boat, the *George Scott*, was sent down from London by rail to Wareham in 1866: 'She was a standard self-righting craft, 30 feet long, pulling ten oars, and was provided with a carriage even though the tracks of the neighbouring area were devious and steep and it would have entailed a long hard journey to any other landing place. As if to emphasise the remoteness of the Pool, the George Scott was first taken to Swanage for her christening by Lady Augusta Freemantle, sister of the Earl of Eldon' (Graham Farr: *Wreck and Rescue on the Dorset Coast*, p 83). The lifeboat station at Chapman's Pool enjoyed only a short life. It was closed down in the 1880s 'because there was no settlement near the water to provide men for the boat with the speed that an emergency demanded' (Rodney Legg: *Purbeck Island*, p 66). In 1920 the nearest lifeboats were stationed at Weymouth in the west and Swanage in the east.

The Inquiry

Second Day - Thursday, 6 May 1920 - Afternoon (continued)

WILLIAM CHAPE (Coastguard at St Alban's Head), examined by Mr Pilcher, said he was on duty on the night of 9/10 January. At 9.20 p.m. he was advised by the Kimmeridge coastguard of the proximity of a steamer 'close in'. He kept her under observation. He could see both her red and green lights. Her lights came slowly on until 10 p.m. when they seemed to stop. She made no signals. At 11 p.m. he received a message from Portland, via Lulworth, that she was aground and that a tug was being sent to her assistance. He informed his chief officer. Witness had not thought the ship was aground, as she showed full navigation lights and made no signals of distress. The weather was misty and rainy, a moderate sea was running and the wind was from the south west, blowing 20 mph. After his relief (Scullard) came at midnight, they called the ship up using the Morse lamp, asking what ship she was. The ship answered, *'Treveal*. Calcutta to Dundee. Ashore hard and fast.' She asked if there was a landing place near and witness's relief signalled, 'Yes, straight inshore, but better wait until daylight if possible.' There was nothing to make witness think there was any danger. The ship was still burning full navigation lights and had made no signals of distress when he went off watch at 3 a.m. At 9 a.m. he came out again. Chief Officer Keeley told him to look out for boats coming from the ship. The weather was thick and he could not see the *Treveal*'s position. It was not until about midday that he heard that the boats were in Chapman's Pool.

Examined by Mr Cunliffe: He could have given a warning signal to the ship when she was approaching the Head, but he did not realise she was as near as she later proved to be. As the ship kept her navigation lights up, he thought her captain knew where he was. Witness thought he might be waiting for a pilot or the tide. After learning that a tug was coming, and seeing the sea to be moderate, witness turned in without anxiety.

Mr Cunliffe: Is it part of the duty of coastguards when a vessel is ashore to notify the lifeboat?

Witness: Yes.

Mr Cunliffe: Was that ever done to your knowledge?

Witness: No.

By the Court: He first notified Chief Officer Keeley that the ship was aground at 11 p.m., after receiving the message from Portland.

JOHN SMITH WRIGHT (Coastguard Divisional Officer, stationed at Swanage), examined by Mr Pilcher, said his district included the stations at Kimmeridge, Lulworth and St Alban's Head. The first message Swanage coastguard station received concerning the *Treveal* was at 11.13 p.m. on 9 January from St Alban's Head. Witness first had personal knowledge of this message at 8.40 the following morning. The message stated that there was a steamer ashore, that she was showing no distress signals and that a tug was being sent to her assistance. Witness asked if the rocket apparatus had been sent out but was told the ship was too far away from the shore for the apparatus to be used. He asked if the lifeboat had been informed and was told that it had. Witness said he first heard of the loss of life from St Alban's Head: he thought it was an officer from Kimmeridge who spoke; and he also spoke to Mr Piercy. Witness proceeded to Worth Matravers by motor with blankets etc, and found seven survivors in a cottage. Witness said that the coastguards did not receive the urgent message, 'For God's sake send assistance,' stated by the *Treveal*'s chief engineer to have been sent by wireless about midnight.

Examined by Mr Cunliffe: He thought it was a matter of opinion whether the volunteer life-saving company should have been called out. He trusted in the station officer's discretion. Witness thought it was not necessary to consider calling out the volunteer company when the ship first struck or until the vessel had asked for assistance. In a situation where the rocket apparatus would be of no use it did not necessarily mean that it might not be prudent to have the volunteer company standing by. Witness agreed that it was the duty of coastguards, as intimated in the coastguard regulations, to immediately inform the lifeboat authorities of a ship ashore. He was not in a position to say whether the neglect to do so was a serious breach of discipline. The matter had been reported to the Admiralty.

Examined by Mr Wilkinson: He thought it was conceivable that with a rising tide and a westerly wind the *Treveal* might have lifted off the Ledge and drifted onto St Alban's Head, and the rocket apparatus would then have been required there. It could have been operated by the four coastguards. Witness said that lifelines could have been taken down to Chapman's Pool in three quarters of an hour. The rocket apparatus would have taken three or four hours.

(The Court adjourned.)

Third Day - Friday, 7 May 1920 - Morning

JOHN SMITH WRIGHT (Coastguard Divisional Officer, stationed at Swanage), recalled and re-examined by Mr Cunliffe, stated that the coastguard station at Bottom, near Chapman's Pool, was closed about 10 years ago.

Mr Cunliffe: In the 'Channel Pilot', the latest edition, I believe, it is stated that there is a coastguard station in Kimmeridge Bay and a detachment at Bottom. If the master of the *Treveal*, on looking at his chart, had referred to the 'Channel Pilot' he might have been distinctly under the impression that in going to Chapman's Pool he was going to a spot where he would meet with assistance?

Witness agreed, and also agreed that it would be the proper course for the captain to refer to the 'Channel Pilot'. Witness could not understand why, in the amendments to the 'Channel Pilot', no reference was made to the discontinuance of the station at Bottom.

By the Court: Strictly speaking the Kimmeridge coastguards, not the St Alban's coastguards, were responsible for Chapman's Pool.

Mr Cunliffe: You said yesterday that you had absolute confidence in the station officer at St Alban's Head?

Witness: I said I trusted in his discretion.

Mr Cunliffe: We know one thing was not in his discretion: the calling out of the lifeboat. That is not in his discretion. Had you been in the position of the station officer at St Alban's Head, would you have taken a different course from the one he adopted?

Mr Pilcher: Before that question is answered, I ask whether it is reasonable to ask this officer to pass judgment upon his subordinate?

Mr Warner (to Mr Cunliffe): You want an expression of opinion?

Mr Cunliffe: Yes.

Mr Pilcher: If the court thinks it right I do not raise an objection.

Mr Wilkinson then objected to the question: it was not for this officer to criticise the action of a subordinate.

Mr Cunliffe replied that the witness was an expert.

A Member of the Court: The court wish to be enlightened as to what was the proper thing to do.

Mr Cunliffe: I will put it in this way: Had you been there during the whole of this night what would you have done under the circumstances appearing in the evidence?

Mr Pilcher: The circumstances are not proved yet.

Mr Cunliffe said he was forced to say - he did not like to say it - that he much regretted that counsel should take up this position, because the court was dealing now with questions which were rather more than questions of professional reputation. The public was particularly jealous of any suggestion that his learned friends were trying in any way to shield a Government department or officers of a Government department. It appeared to him that they were endeavouring to do so.

The President: I cannot agree with that.

Mr Pilcher said it was extremely regrettable that counsel for the shipowners should make such a statement. The Board of Trade were laying all the facts before the court and had nothing to keep back. If he thought a question improper, however, he was entitled to say so and to submit his reasons to the court.

Mr Wilkinson said that the Admiralty were not shielding anybody or anything. He was only protesting against the question.

A Member of the Court asked to be reminded what was the question Mr Cunliffe wished to put to the witness.

The Clerk of the Court: The question Mr Cunliffe wants put is this: 'Had you been there under the circumstances you have heard proved, what would you have done?'

Witness: Not having heard all the evidence as to the circumstances which existed at St Alban's Head, I would rather not express an opinion.

The President asked Mr Cunliffe to proceed with his next question.

Mr Cunliffe said he had no further questions.

By Mr Pilcher: It was in the discretion of a chief coastguard officer to send a patrol in any direction if he could spare the men.

The St Alban's Head coastguard station was described by Nina Warner Hooke as 'a naval punishment station' ('Avoidable Loss' in *Dorset*, No 70, p 10). There is no reference in the records of the Coastguard Museum to the station ever having such a status. Museum manager Mr K Anthony Ellis did, however, speculate: 'I am sure that within the Navy's Coastguard, there were unpopular and hard to man stations which would be offered to miscreants and perpetrators of minor offences on disciplinary moves.'

Just as the parish of Worth Matravers had thrust upon it eccentric vicars, who appear to have been given the remote parish to keep them well out of harm's way, so a posting to St Alban's Head was not one, perhaps, that a coastguard would chose, given a choice. It was isolated and exposed even by the usual standards of coastguard stations. When there was a real 'blow' the coastguards often had to crawl to the 'look out'; any man who stood up risked being blown 400 feet to his death. Crossing the 'Plain' from the village you can lean your whole weight into the wind without falling.

The St Alban's Head coastguard houses were in a solid terrace of four. The rooms were large, as if to give the coastguards 'spread' from their poky watch box. At night the pressure burner lamps hissed, rebuking the dense shadows. It was, perhaps, a last fling at a time gone by that when the station closed in 1950 a fortune in 'rubbish' was thrown over the cliff: lamps (all styles, shapes and sizes), bedsteads with brass knobs, knick-knacks bought from itinerant suitcase salesmen ...

But there was real antiquity at St Alban's Head - something far older than the Board of Trade, Ministry of Shipping, Admiralty or Department of Trade: the chapel. Shaped like a cardinal's hat, it is rough hewn, as if from rubble round about, and except for the door there is not a chip of wood in the whole building. It is dedicated to St Aldhealm, first Bishop of Sherborne. There is a local legend which says that in 1140 a bride and groom were sailing round the headland watched by the bride's father. A storm suddenly arose, the boat capsized and the newly-weds were drowned. The desolate father is said to have built the chapel to their memory, and a beacon was always to be kept burning to warn other sailors. The chapel has had a mixed history; as much used to dung from passing cows and trapezium cobwebs as free-floating summer prayers and fresh flowers. It was sometimes used as a wishing chapel. Young girls would drop a pin into a hole in the centre pillar and wish for the husband of their choice. Dora Lander was taken by her mother for just that purpose. In keeping with the aloofness of the promontory, the chapel does not appear to have been in ecclesiastical connection with the parish of Worth Matravers (or with any religious establishment).

What solace was there for a man and his family posted to St Alban's coastguard station? It was especially hard on the children who had to walk to the village school every day, through what was known as the 'Ruts': huge tracks left by horses and wagons. In summer they would buzz with flies - though in summer there must have been some enchantment walking home across the Plain. Mushrooms, ranging from huge 'horse' mushrooms to tiny pink 'buttons', puff balls to be kicked sky high, a fox tiptoeing along a hedgerow, an occasional adder to tease and kill, butterflies, as elusive of capture as the shadow of a passing cloud ... and at last home ... the path marked by large, white stones, in case of sudden fog which could come down in minutes.

All drinking water had to be carried to the station from the village well, but groceries were delivered by Mr Smith of Langton Matravers; the Pushmans at Worth Matravers post office and grocery store didn't get a look in. There was one vegetable absent from the coastguards' shopping list: potatoes. The coastguards dug early potatoes at Ring Bum Gardens - a freak place that seems never to be touched by frost. Thus, the coastguard station was 'well away' from Worth Matravers village, with its own climate, manners and mores.

On the night of Friday, 9 January 1920, while Worth Matravers villagers shut fast doors and windows against the night, snuffed out candles on mantelshelves and climbed stairs to chilly bedrooms, out on the cliffs, in the sentinel lookout boxes, sharp eyes swept the dark expanse of the English Channel.

The coast between Weymouth Bay and Swanage Bay, a distance of about 30 miles, is formidable, consisting of towering cliffs, and rocky coves and inlets. Any ship driven against the cliffs is doomed. In the early hours of Friday, 6 January 1786, the *Halsewell*, an East Indiaman with 242 people on board, was smashed to pieces against the cliffs between Winspit and Seacombe, with the loss of 166 lives. As dangerous as the cliffs themselves are the hazards which lurk offshore. At several points invisible reefs run far out into the Channel. There is one at Peveril Point, where a whole Viking fleet came to grief in King Alfred's reign, and there is the Kimmeridge Ledge, angling out from Kimmeridge Bay for some miles in the direction of St Alban's Head, causing ships of deep draught to give the Head a wide berth when passing up or down Channel. It is well known to sailors as a graveyard for many a fine vessel, and just how greatly it is feared can be judged by what Captain Kemp had said about it during my interview with him at St Ives.

Q. What did you know about the Kimmeridge Ledge?

A. I didn't go that far in near the bloody Kimmeridge Ledge. I wasn't going to look at the Kimmeridge Ledge.

Q. So you gave it a wide berth as they say?

A. You bet your life.

The *Treveal* steamed up Channel from the direction of Portland, passing coastguard station after coastguard station; watched by the watchers. She should have been 10 miles out from the shore; she wasn't. In the words of George Chillingworth, chief coastguard officer at Kimmeridge, 'she was about five miles out of her proper course' and 'had no business to be where she was.' St Alban's Head was warned of a steamer 'close in'. The coastguard on watch there, William Chape, 'kept her under observation.' Still the watchers watched. The *Treveal*, in fact, was already aground, hard and fast, on the Kimmeridge Ledge. Allan Woolcock, the veteran cook, who had never been shipwrecked before, and who was in his bunk when the ship struck, had come up on deck to see the dark mass of St Alban's Head towering up off the bow - a sheer 400-foot cliff with no room for even a seagull's foot to gain a hold. At the cliff's edge was the chapel, empty as a mouth agape for prayer. In another age a sailor - perhaps away for years, with only his captain as his God - would, on seeing the chapel, make a blessing on his voyage and, on his return, offer up praises for safe deliverance from the perils of the sea. The crew of the *Treveal*, however, were not looking to the chapel for succour but to the coastguard station next to it.

The Inquiry

Third Day - Friday, 7 May 1920 - Morning (continued)

FREDERICK KEELEY (Coastguard Chief Petty Officer at St Alban's Head), examined by Mr Pilcher, said his full complement was one petty officer and five ratings, but at the time in question he had two men on leave, thus having but four beside himself. The four were doing six-hour watches each. Witness stated that he was in bed at 11 p.m. on 9 January when he received a telephone message from the man on watch (Chape), stating that a message had been received from Portland, or from Portland via Lulworth, that a ship was ashore near St Alban's Head and that a Government tug was being sent to her assistance. Witness instructed the man on the watch to inform the divisional officer at Swanage and to keep strict watch on the vessel, to see whether she altered her position or gave any signals of distress; also, when the watch was changed at midnight, to signal to ask what the vessel was and what was her condition. Witness dressed and went out on the cliffs. With his binoculars he could see a faint outline of the ship. She was burning full navigation lights and looked as if she was lying off. She was showing no signals of distress. There was a moderate breeze, WSW, and a constant drizzle of rain. Shortly after midnight communication with the ship was established by Morse lamp. The ship signalled that she was hard and fast and asked if there was a safe landing place. The man on watch (Scullard) reported this to witness and witness dictated the reply: 'Yes, straight inshore from you, but better wait until daylight if possible.' Witness stated that at 4.50 a.m. another message was received from the ship asking them to inform Portland that the tug had not yet arrived. This was done and the reply received from Portland was that the tug *Pilot* had left at 12.15 a.m. and must have arrived. Shortly afterwards there was a message from Portland that the *Pilot* had returned, having failed to find the ship and having no signalman on board, but was leaving again immediately. Witness gave instructions for this message to be sent to the *Treveal*. His men tried to signal her for two hours, between 5 and 7 a.m., but she failed to respond. Witness said he did not give any instructions for his men to patrol Chapman's Pool. His station was a war signal station and, with only four men at the station at the time, he could not spare any for patrol work. In any case his patrol extended in the other direction, towards Anvil Point. Witness stated that shortly after 7 a.m. he saw a tug a mile and a half to the windward of the *Treveal*, lying off. The wind and sea were getting up a little. The telephone between the Head and Swanage was out of order between 1 and 5.30 a.m. At the latter hour a message was sent for the attention of the divisional officer at Swanage that the *Treveal* was not in danger, but that the tug had not yet arrived. At 8 a.m. a further message was dispatched that the tug was now standing by. Witness stated that at about 8.30 a.m. flags were visible on the *Treveal* but they could not at first read them because the weather was so thick. At 8.40 a.m. the signals were deciphered as: AG ('I must abandon vessel'); NR ('I want assistance. Please remain by me'); and PYL ('Keep as close as you can to pick up my people'). The first two signals were urgent and important but were not distress signals. The third signal, according to the international code, was not an urgent one. Witness thought the signals were directed at the tug. He could not see anything of the tug at the time. The wind was getting very strong with heavy rain squalls. He did not see or hear rocket distress signals.

(*The Coroner*: Can you explain why you could not hear the signals which were heard here (Worth Matravers)? *Witness*: The only explanation I can give is that there were heavy seas breaking on the beach; and the rain squalls and the wind drove the sounds up Chapman's Pool and through the valley. (Inquest))

Witness said he gave instructions for the *Treveal*'s flag signals to be notified to the divisional officer at Swanage, the Kimmeridge coastguard, and the Weymouth coastguard for transmission to the secretary of the Weymouth lifeboat.

(JOHN SMITH WRIGHT (Coastguard Divisional Officer, stationed at Swanage) was recalled to explain the method of communication with the Weymouth lifeboat: The Weymouth coastguards would receive the message via Lulworth or Portland and they would inform the secretary of the Weymouth lifeboat. The secretary was not on the telephone.)

FREDERICK KEELEY (examination by Mr Pilcher continued): Witness instructed his men to keep a strict watch on the *Treveal* to see if any boats left her, but nothing was seen. Heavy rain squalls obscured the vessel at times. If he had seen the boats leave he would have sent men down to Chapman's Pool with lifelines and lifebelts. At about 10 a.m. a fisherman came up and said he had come from Chapman's Pool. Witness asked him if he had seen anything of any boats there, and he distinctly said he had seen nothing. The first witness heard of the landing at Chapman's Pool was at 12.30 p.m. when a petty officer from Kimmeridge came up and reported that there were seven survivors and many bodies washing in. Witness sent two men down at once. The reason he did not notify the lifeboat any earlier was because the *Treveal* was showing full navigation lights and, as her deck lights were burning, he thought she was under steam and might get off the Ledge on the rising tide in the morning. If she had put out her navigation lights and hoisted two red lights on her mast he would have known she was in distress. When he received the message from Portland that the ship was ashore and that a tug was being sent to her assistance he did not think it was part of his duty to interfere with the arrangements. He considered the question of calling out the volunteer life-saving company but thought it unnecessary as up until 8.40 a.m. he had no reason to believe the ship was in particular danger. He did not dispatch the rocket apparatus to Chapman's Pool because he thought that if the *Treveal* did come off the Ledge she might be driven onto the Head. In that case the rocket apparatus would have been of real service, whereas it would have been useless at the Pool, the ship being far out of range, and if he had fired it over the lifeboats the line would have cut the men to pieces. *Examined by Mr Cunliffe*: If the watchman had considered the *Treveal* was standing into danger he could have sent the usual signal. When witness did not have his full complement of men for patrol work, there was no arrangement for supplementing his men from the volunteer company.

Mr Cunliffe: Did you think the inquiry for a landing place showed that the vessel was in danger?

Witness: No, I thought it was a precautionary measure which any good captain would take when in such circumstances.

By Mr Cunliffe: He did not in the least think that at almost any time the crew of the *Treveal* would have to put out in boats. He was trying to get a reply from the ship as to her condition and the intentions of the crew from 5 till 7 a.m., but could get no reply.

(The Court adjourned for lunch.)

Afternoon

FREDERICK KEELEY (Coastguard Chief Petty Officer at St Alban's Head), recalled and examined by Mr Wilkinson, said he understood a ship to be in distress when she showed signals, not merely because she was ashore. He did not receive any signal of distress whatever. The *Treveal* never showed a black ball and flag. If the ship had informed him that they were going to land at Chapman's Pool he would have had men on the beach to receive them. He thought he could have directed them to a safe landing place and that it would not have been necessary to use any apparatus. If they had landed at daylight, as he suggested, they would have had 150 yards of a good beach to land on.

By the Court: If the *Treveal* had sent out any signals of distress during the night he would have had no hesitation in calling out the lifeboat.

THOMAS SCULLARD (Coastguard Petty Officer at St Alban's Head), examined by Mr Pilcher, said he went on duty at midnight on the night of 9/10 January and saw the lights of the ship. He corroborated the evidence as to the messages sent and received during the night. He went off watch at 6 a.m. and came back out at about 9 a.m. He saw the flag signals on the *Treveal*. He had not imagined the vessel to be in any danger before he saw the signals. The weather was getting worse. He did not see boats leave the *Treveal*.

Examined by Mr Cunliffe: He was of opinion that if he had been sent down to Chapman's Pool and seen the boats he could not have done anything, except wade in and try and rescue men. He heard no distress

94

rockets.

Examined by Mr Wilkinson: The message from the *Treveal* asking when the tug was coming led the coastguards to believe that the crew were relying on the tug's assistance and were not in imminent danger. He saw the tug at 9 a.m. She appeared to be closing a little on the *Treveal*, but seemed to be making heavy weather. Witness did not think the tug got within a mile of the *Treveal*.

GEORGE BUTT (Coastguard at St Alban's Head), examined by Mr Pilcher, said he came on duty at 4.30 a.m. on 10 January. He first saw the tug at about 7.30 a.m. It was about two miles from the *Treveal*. Visibility was poor and the tug might have come within a quarter of a mile of the *Treveal* without his seeing it. He corroborated the evidence as to the difficulty of reading the flag signals on the *Treveal*, and of a watch being kept for boats leaving her, which they did not see.

Examined by Mr Cunliffe: If the *Treveal* had put up the usual distress signal in the morning, they would have recognised it at once and could have taken immediate action.

EUGENE MOULAN (Coastguard at St Alban's Head), examined by Mr Pilcher, said he sent the message for the Weymouth lifeboat after the flag signals on the *Treveal* were read at 8.40 a.m. on 10 January. He saw the tug at daybreak two miles south of the *Treveal*. He could not understand how the two boats left the *Treveal* without being seen.

GEORGE CHILLINGWORTH (Coastguard Chief Petty Officer at Kimmeridge), examined by Mr Pilcher, said he observed the *Treveal* making from the direction of the Portland Breakwater on the night of 9 January. At 8.40 p.m. she was about three miles west of his station. At 9.20 p.m. when east of his station she altered course a little towards the sea and the St Alban's Head coastguard was advised of her presence. At 9.40 p.m. St Alban's reported that the vessel was approaching slowly. Witness heard that the ship was ashore at 11.30 p.m. and gave his men instructions to keep a sharp look out. After midnight she could not be seen from his station. At 9.15 a.m., when he heard that the *Treveal* was being abandoned, he sent two men (Hurden and Titcombe) along the coast to render any assistance they could. Chapman's Pool was about four miles distant, over very difficult ground. His men reached the Pool too late to be of any use. At about 12.30 p.m. one of them (Hurden) reported from St Alban's Head that there were seven survivors.

Examined by Mr Cunliffe: When the *Treveal* passed his station she was about five miles out of her proper course. After she had passed he lost her red light, and a few minutes after he saw it again. She had no business to be where she was, but he thought she was too far out to have gone ashore at that time.

Mr Cunliffe: Had you ever seen a steamship so close inshore before?

Witness: No.

Mr Cunliffe: It must have been a very alarming spectacle to those on St Alban's Head?

Witness: I don't know about that.

By Mr Cunliffe: Vessels bound from Weymouth up Channel generally kept 10 miles away from the shore. There was no landing place between witness's station and Chapman's Pool. It was a custom in the coastguard service to flash a signal to ships that were standing into danger, but it did not appear to be necessary when the *Treveal* passed his station; she was steering fairly parallel with the coast.

By the Court: He telephoned St Alban's Head because the *Treveal* seemed to be steering an erratic course. Before she passed his station she was steering very steady. After she passed she altered her course towards the sea, and then came in again. (Witness pointed out to the court the apparent course on a chart.)

(The Court adjourned.)

It might be said that the Kimmeridge Ledge is the most important character in the story of the loss of the *Treveal*. How the character of the Ledge was perceived by the human characters, dictated so much of what was done or wasn't done. Chief Officer Keeley at St Alban's Head thought that during the night, although the *Treveal* was ashore hard and fast on the Ledge, she was not in distress; Henry Burden, secretary of the Poole lifeboat, thought that any vessel on the Ledge was in danger from the time it struck, and the lives of the crew unquestionably. Chief Officer Keeley thought that the *Treveal* might have come off the Ledge in the morning and been driven onto the Head; to Frank Lander's knowledge no ship once on the Ledge had come off again. Captain Paynter wirelessed for a tug when the *Treveal* ran aground, and eight or nine hours later still hoped to save the ship, asking for a salvage steamer and lighter; Alfred Spranklin, coxswain of the Weymouth lifeboat, said that a vessel on the Ledge for more than one tide in bad weather was doomed.

What, then, of the character of the Kimmeridge Ledge? It had been there, as a vague presence, exuding danger, all my life; but what was it in concrete terms?

First, I went to Kimmeridge foreshore, where great cubes of stone are strewn over the beach as if expertly split by quarrymen. Beyond are the ledges themselves (the Kimmeridge Ledge is not a single, continuous feature), cracked like crazy paving, just beneath the surface of the sea - reaching out like a witch's finger towards St Alban's Head. Geologically, the *Treveal* was stuck fast on the Corralian strata, a Jurassic formation, overlaying the Oxfordian. This rises at an angle, east to west, bed over bed, like the teeth of a saw.

I next decided to go over the Ledge. Boarding Nick Ford's fishing boat, I was taken to the spot where the *Treveal* had struck. We drifted a while then, suddenly, beneath us was a spine of stone and waving seaweed: the dreaded Kimmeridge Ledge. I felt I could have leant over and touched it, so shallow was the water. We were about a mile away from Chapman's Pool, but only half a mile out from the shore just east of Freshwater Steps. Captain Kemp had said when I interviewed him:

'The story in St Ives was that on the Sunday morning the *Treveal* was standing right up on the Ledge, and you could have walked out ashore.'

'Almost, along the Ledge ...' I had replied, and an incident from my childhood had suddenly come into my mind like a cork popping up from the sea.

One day at Chapman's Pool a few local boys watched some fishermen plod up the steep hillside, turning every now and then to look back down at the Pool, to see if any young 'varmints' were hanging around their skiffs. They would not be back for two days. The boys had only to wait. One boy was new; from London. The fishermen gone, the boys got aboard a skiff, pushed off and rowed out to sea - a sparkling sea, with not a twitch of an evil current. The new boy looked over the side.

'I'm going to get out and have a paddle ...'

So, like a benign sea monster, the Kimmeridge Ledge allowed a boy to paddle along its weed-waving spine a mile from shore.

I was not going to get out of Nick Ford's boat and do the same, but I was going to walk along the Ledge. For this I had to wait for the next low spring tide. I walked out. I felt an intruder in a place once the habitat of dinosaurs and toothed birds. I went as far as I could, anxiously watching for the freak wave that might come crashing along the Ledge. Were it possible for a giant plug to have been pulled, a lower landscape of undulation would have been revealed: steep banks, valleys, holes in holes, all of a slither, gaps, wherein lay shingle, large boulders around which the tide would swirl; and I would be standing at the highest peak, over which the sea would rise back and bubble like a school of basking whales. I knew the time of low tide, and on the minute the tide turned and began to trickle in, long before the green seaweed had dried out. I hastened back to the shore, the sea at my heels, closing over the Ledge once more.

It was dark by the time I reached the top of Chapman's Pool Hill and looked back. The Kimmeridge Ledge was again just a vague presence; a lurking danger. I was leaning against the old stone wall which my grandfather and Horace Piercy had sheltered behind as they looked for a ship in distress. The *Treveal* had been on the Ledge all night. It seemed to me she was like a dying animal - none of her kind would come near her.

What was the atmosphere aboard the *Treveal* during the long night of waiting for assistance which never came? A ship's crew is a microcosm of mankind. When the flurry of activity in the first hours after going aground had abated, would the sea lawyer have started stoking where fires were hottest in men's minds? Would the lawyer have set off the moaner? The moaner the joker? The joker the evangelist, who would sing 'Drear was the voyage, sailor, now almost o'er; Safe within the lifeboat, sailor, pull for the shore' - until someone threw a boot at his head? Would men have re-read their letters? Smoked and sipped a strong, sweet 'brew'? Prayed? ... Said little?

Chief Engineer Thirkell, in an interview with the press soon after the disaster, said that 'to a man' the crew stood by the ship till the last; but a slightly different picture emerged at the inquiry. There seems to have been a division between those above deck and those below. Optimism was highest on the bridge, judged by the wireless messages Captain Paynter sent out, and by what Third Officer Donald said in evidence at the inquiry. It was, of course, in the officers' interest - and Captain Paynter's in particular - that the ship should not be lost. Among the sailors, too - all Cornishmen, with an allegiance to company and captain; and some of whom had been on the watch and seen nothing before the ship struck - there was the desire to believe that the ship could be saved. Able Seaman Winterbottom, for example, said at the inquiry that he did not think the crew were in danger, and that the men were not nervous at all: 'they were all right.'

Below deck, though, where the ship was filling with water, and where the noise of her straining and 'making noises showing that she was being damaged' was all the more intense, the atmosphere was different. No blame could be attached to a fireman for a ship going aground. No fireman could be persuaded to stand by the ship through any sense of local loyalty. Down below, the men wanted away as soon as possible. The cook, Woolcock, noticed that they became anxious to leave about midnight. Chief Engineer Thirkell admitted at the inquiry that they were very much upset, asking when the lifeboat was coming. Thirkell himself, with his long experience, was 'personally convinced of the danger during the night', but, presumably for the captain's sake, seems to have done his best to pacify the men below - toing and froing from the bridge, returning with encouraging news: the wireless operator had sent out a message, 'For God's sake send assistance.'

Dawn broke, the *Treveal* split along her side and Captain Paynter gave the order to abandon ship.

Chapter 7

Many people have a fear of drowning. When a young man, I myself, with two companions, nearly drowned off Egmont Point, an outcrop of jagged rocks on the west side of Chapman's Pool. We had decided, the night before, to try to save some lobster pots off the Kimmeridge Ledge as the wind was 'getting up'. In the village the sea could be heard as a continuous groundswell. Arriving at the Pool we saw the waves were a dirty brown colour, as if some sea god had raked the muddy shoreline. Our skiff was little more than a tin bath, driven by an outboard engine. We hauled the pots - two for each life - and made for home. Just off Freshwater Steps the engine spluttered and stopped. If we could pull round Egmont Point with our oars we could, with good luck, cross the bay with our six empty pots. For the first time, without the noise of the engine, we heard what the sailors of the *Treveal* had heard: the terrible roar of the sea pounding against rocks. Slowly the tide took us towards them - and then a few surges and we were within the dreadful rockery. The sea swirled us like flotsam, sluiced us down the length of one huge rock then lifted us over another - in such a confined place we could not use our oars. Suddenly, by chance, rated by some as a miracle, we were tossed back into open water, and rowed 'all of a shake' for the safety of the Dock. Drowning at Egmont Point would have been death by pounding. Those of the *Treveal*'s crew who drifted westward had their clothes ripped from their bodies and their flesh torn from their bones by contact with the sharp rocks of Egmont.

I returned to Chapman's Pool a few days after my fortuitous escape, when another 'blow' was on. The sea cascaded angrily around the foreshore and the sky mazily obscured a pale, yellow sun. All kinds of rubbish littered the beach: the one-legged man's shoe, brushes with a few bristles, a mop-head, packing cases from Hull, cuttlefish, a few oranges, contraceptives, bottles, a punctured football, a large blue drum with a skull and cross-bones on it. Perhaps I needed to go there again, for no man has his soul intact who has not borrowed from it the hour of his death. For many years after that Chapman's Pool held little pleasure for me - no doubt I had residual anxiety about my near-death experience. It was vanquished in an odd way. One afternoon in late summer I looked down on the cove and saw a body washing back and forth on the shoreline. There was no one on the beach. The body was clothed, as far as I could see, in a black uniform and its arms and legs kept crossing and uncrossing as it rolled in the surf. I approached it closer, almost tiptoeing, dreading what I should see ... then I caught sight of a tail. It was a young bullock that had fallen over the cliff. Thereafter, for some reason, not even the deepest dusk or roughest day could cause a ripple of anxiety in my psyche.

For my grandfather, Frank Lander, the memory of what he saw in Chapman's Pool on the morning of 10 January 1920 would never be exorcised; it would be quietly endured. In the press, in the aftermath of the disaster, the role of the 'local fisherman' was eclipsed by that of the 'HEROIC CLERGYMAN'. At the inquest, particularly, but also at the later inquiry, the evidence of the educated, articulate and outspoken curate was given with gusto and reported in detail. In many newspapers 'the fisherman Lander' merely 'corroborated': quiet and modest, he had no axe to grind. Thus, Horace Piercy's rescue work is well-documented, while my grandfather's part is largely marginalised in the recorded history. Indeed, when the *Bournemouth Daily Echo* (12 January 1970) remembered the 50th anniversary of the *Treveal* disaster, Frank Lander was forgotten altogether. Only after a number of readers' letters (including one from Frank's son, Sid) did the *Echo* (2 February 1970) acknowledge that 'there were in fact two heroes.' In the circumstances, I make no apology for giving an account of the events of 10 January principally from my grandfather's point of view.

Even though the coastguards did not call out the volunteer company there was, in the aftermath of the *Treveal* disaster, the vague implication that the villagers of Worth Matravers had somehow let the crew of the *Treveal* down. Why was Frank Lander the only person to hear the distress rockets? The rockets having been heard by him, surely the news went round from door to door like news of a death? Why, then, didn't the whole village turn out and make down to Chapman's Pool?

It was a wild January morning. Few people would have been walking abroad. Those who were out would have had their heads down against the wind and rain. In fact, people other than Frank did hear the distress rockets, but did not recognise them for what they were. Charlie Newman, landlord of the Square and Compass Inn and captain of the volunteer life-saving company, for example, heard what he thought was the Tank Corps at gun practice, at Bovington Camp, 10 miles away. Worth Matravers was a village used to bangs - from the cliff quarries to naval gunfire. Before the First World War dreadnought class ships used to practice along the south coast - bang, bang. 'Much more of this and we shall have rain' the villagers would say. They were used to commotion. Only Frank Lander, a man with very sharp senses, who happened to be working in a shed open to the south, heard the *Treveal*'s rockets 'plain as day'. The news did go round the village but, perhaps, the time of year and the sale of the village a few months earlier, inclined some towards a sense of privacy rather than community: they retreated behind doors hung with coats, let the curtains bide drawn, the dog whine and the chickens stay cooped up. There was no signal from the coastguards, which would have guaranteed them their few shillings for turning out, and for those who had just bought cottages money was tighter than ever. They had not heard the distress rockets themselves and Chapman's Pool was some distance from the village over difficult, and in the prevailing weather, almost impossible terrain.

Frank Lander alone had heard the rockets with his own ears and call out or no call out felt it his duty to investigate. He dashed in from the shed, grabbing a raincoat from a peg. His wife, Jane, hadn't time even to ask what had happened. She heard the words 'Chapman's Pool', then, closing the door, he was gone. Had he heard of someone in danger? Sid, their son, a tall, strong man, was away at the time, working in Swanage. Was Frank going alone to Chapman's Pool? Was he going to risk his own life? She looked at her two daughters, Daisy Kate, white as a starched collar, just recovered from Spanish flu, ostracised by many, and Dora, village school teacher, tiny and brave, running her finger along the table cloth. Why *was* Frank going to Chapman's Pool?

Frank, meanwhile, wondered at his own temerity, venturing out in hurricane force winds, when there was not even a signal from the St Alban's Head coastguards. Frank's neighbour, Edwin Bower, was 'knocked up', but refused to come out. Edwin was sunny side and sour side. He sang boisterously for pints at the Square and Compass, often banging for order: 'I'm not a bloody sideshow.' Yet, for a living, he quarried and fished alone. Frank went on. On the way to Weston Farm he met Horace Piercy, walking back to the village with his milk. What Horace might have done if he had not met Frank is a matter of conjecture. For sure, Frank was committed to going to Chapman's Pool come what may. In the event, they chanced to meet and there was a brief exchange of words:

Horace: Where are you going, Frank?

Frank: Chapman's Pool. I heard rockets fired.

Horace: May I come with you?

- and the two men set out. Without them there might have been total loss of life at Chapman's Pool.

Once off the road they went along the cliff path, trying to run but stumbling against the wind and gusts of rain. At times all light was shut from the sky. On reaching a stone wall both men flung themselves down to gain some respite. Frank removed some loose stones to make a peephole and squinted through.

'There she is,' he cried. 'She's on the Ledge.'

A hand was on his shoulder and the curate pressed his eye to the hole. He saw the stricken ship.

What was to be done? The two men debated whether to go back to the village to get more help or to press on. They concluded that the ship must have been seen by the St Alban's Head coastguards, and decided to continue to the Pool. Over the rickety stile they went and down the steep and slippery Fishermen's Path - Horace's brogues and Frank's stout boots pounding in unison, on and off the muddy path as they tried to keep their balance. Reaching level ground, they ran between tall, sodden bramble bushes; and it was then that they saw, for the first time, the ship's lifeboats, bottom up, some men clinging to them and others in the sea, struggling, choking and drowning. Frank and Horace, slithering and sliding down the ravine which lead to the beach, saw one of the boats lifted clean out of the sea and smashed to matchwood against the rocks to the west of the cove. Down they ran, to Chief Engineer Thirkell and Able Seaman Winterbottom, who had already hauled themselves out of the foaming cauldron. Winterbottom, the more alert of the two exhausted men, pointed mutely to the figure of the cook, Woolcock, being rolled over and over in the surf, and Frank and Horace hauled him up the beach to safety.

The behaviour of the two rescuers thereafter was determined by their respective characters and experiences. Frank, on the one hand, knew little of death, but all about the sea and the particular hazards of Chapman's Pool; Horace, on the other, knew Chapman's Pool only as a place for summer picnics, but knew all about death - and had perhaps become reckless in the face of it - as a stretcher-bearer in the First World War. A moment passed in which the pitiful sight of the drowning men was seared in Frank's mind forever and while he desperately assessed the best way to go about trying to save them. Horace, meanwhile, careless for his own safety, rushed out into the sea, an act as likely to produce another victim as to save life. Perhaps he needed Frank as an anchor man, psychologically as well as physically. A huge wave washed him out into the sea and when, by luck, the next brought him back Frank was there to grab him - and a handful of the hair of the sailor he had managed to get a hold of: Third Officer William Donald.

Having experienced the force of the backwash and the shifting shingle underfoot, Horace made no further dashes into the sea, but was floated out on the end of Frank's strong arm (Frank having anchored himself on the beach as best he could) to save three more men, and to pull in the body of Chief Officer Hutchinson. Frank turned the men upside down to drain the water out of them; all were revived except the chief officer. Mont Hooper, Walter Welsh and two women of the village had by now arrived at the Pool. As the men pulled out more bodies the women helped revive and comfort the survivors.

The storm raged on, one of those terrifying winds, which had begun with the air being drawn out of the sky as if Nature was holding its breath ... Then the blow, with sudden strong gusts, each stronger than the last, portending that nothing can stand what will come next. Along the seashore it roared as if a demented pipe-organist was blowing through the deep. Some of the survivors, those who could walk, had already begun the climb up the gully to Hill Bottom; others needed help. They were so few; the dead so many.

The furious waves which washed up the bodies of the Hain crew were under the same power as the sea water I had seen trickle back over the Kimmeridge Ledge after a low tide - and which, for half a century, had washed up the profits against the Hain manor house door. These were trading people and their ships were trading ships. Had they been under sail in earlier days they would have been searching for El Dorado, to dust themselves down in gold dust and become gods on earth.

On 10 January 1920, in the fissure in the middle of the cliff at Chapman's Pool (a great bog of grey, slimy filth, known locally as the 'Lake') a few bulrushes swayed and bobbed in salutary fashion, as if expecting the arrival of a potentate. Instead came a sailor, whose top coat hung off his shoulders and so far down his back that the hem twirled in a kind of tail. Then another, screaming to be left there to die. Others staggered up the gully, exchanging their clothes for a coating of thick mud. Their speech came in gasps - gasps lost in the roaring wind driven like Jehu up the valley. These hideous lumps of crawling clay, dragged along by their rescuers, eventually reached higher ground. Looking up with the lie of the land, they saw - hardly daring to believe they saw - the warm glow of a lamplit window.

The former coastguard cottages at Chapman's Pool, latterly holiday homes, were always empty during the winter months. Not until the first primrose, the first brimstone butterfly and the first adder signalled spring would the owners of the cottages make their appearance. No 4 cottage was home to Mr Darvelle, prep school master; No 3 to the Froud family, wealthy shoeshop owners; No 2 to Mr Gilderdale, prep school master; and No 1 (the former station officer's house) to the Miss Thompsons - three maiden ladies of impeccable good breeding, whose foibles were legion, as, for instance, in insisting that their eggs be from hens that had not been with a cock bird.

Mr Gilderdale, who supplied the *Treveal* survivors with blankets - and who, in the case of one man whose condition resisted orthodox comfort, in desperation held his feet in the oven - is not reported to have given evidence at either the inquests or the inquiry. Add to that his status as an outsider in the village and he becomes a mystery. Why did Mr Gilderdale in 1920, in the very depths of winter, decide to go to inhospitable Chapman's Pool? To get away from it all before the 'hols' were over? To think over his life? It was said at the time, to do some decorating, but who knows. Mr Gilderdale, prep school master was 'at home' to the seven lucky crewmen of the *Treveal*. What manner of man was he? Worth Matravers grocer Mr Pushman didn't like him, marking him as mean since his outburst at the Pushman price of plums: 'Penny each! A disgraceful price to ask for plums, certainly not, sir!' And he was away from the shop back to Chapman's Pool, where at least mushrooms and blackberries were free. By all accounts, though, Mr Gilderdale gave readily of his larder's provisions to the *Treveal* survivors, who, after being immersed in the freezing sea and the gruelling ascent from the beach to the old coastguard cottages, were in desperate need of sustenance.

But had Mr Gilderdale not heard the rockets earlier? It was said that 'the wind drove the sounds up Chapman's Pool and through the valley.' Had he not seen the vessel, close in, with her navigation lights burning all through the night? Was he not abroad on the morning of 10 January? A prep school master might see a storm as great fun, not a million miles away from diving naked into the school plunge pool, but Mr Gilderdale apparently had not ventured out.

However, very bad weather always brought *someone* to the beach in the early hours. In a community of fishermen and men whose working environment was deep darkness (the underground quarries), the very night air could be said to be their element, and there were always those with a lantern ready and their ear tuned to the intensity of a storm. Often they were away, out of sight, before dawn broke. Who, for instance, was the fisherman who Station Officer Keeley said came up to St Alban's

Head at about 10 a.m. on the morning of 10 January, saying he had come from Chapman's Pool and had seen nothing of any boats? Chapman's Pool, a bay with a narrow entrance and a wide basin: a bay of promise, which might roll booty or a corpse ashore - a corpse that might have about it things of value: a loose ring on a frozen finger, coins in a money belt ...

The Treveal wrecked on the Kimmeridge Ledge

Frank Lander and Horace Piercy, looking back from the coastguard cottages to Chapman's Pool, could see the *Treveal*, split in two on the Kimmeridge Ledge - the two halves about 60 feet apart. In the moments of rescue Frank and Horace had been together, on level terms; but afterwards their apartness by social class was soon restored. The newspapers saw to it that that was so, and it was accepted by both men as the 'natural order'. At Swanage Town Hall, Frank and Horace were each presented with the Royal Humane Society's bronze medal and a certificate signed by the Society's president, 'Edward P', afterwards King Edward VIII; the Reverend Piercy alone was presented with a fine oil painting in a gilded frame as well.

Both men, on the morning of 10 January, wondered and voiced their concern as to where the St Alban's Head coastguards were. Each acted according to his nature. Frank, kind, generous, thoughtful, stayed on the beach to pull out the bodies, looking for any lingering signs of life: that was his 'nature'. Horace, a complex man, a Cambridge man, soaked to his skin, ran all the way to the coastguard station at St Alban's Head, to give someone a roasting. It was some feat. The easier path, through the middle cliff, known locally as the 'Wilderness' (the terminus of Lord Eldon's carriage ride) was in 1920 overgrown and strewn with huge boulders. Thus, the exhausted curate would have had to have run along a rough and slippery path to Pier Bottom, then climbed 350 feet to the coastguard station. But that was his 'nature'.

The actions of the two men afterwards were consistent with their actions on the day. Years later, Frank Lander could be found, without fuss or favour, fishing from Chapman's Pool. The wild curate was long gone away.

The Inquiry
Fourth Day - Monday, 10 May 1920 - Morning

(The Court, departing from its previous practice, ordered all witnesses who had not yet been called to leave the room.)

MR PILCHER, referring to the earlier examination of the coastguard divisional officer, Smith Wright, by Mr Cunliffe, pointed out that there was an amendment to the 'Channel Pilot' issued in 1917, stating that the coastguard station at Bottom (near Chapman's Pool) was closed.

GEORGE CHILLINGWORTH (Coastguard Chief Petty Officer at Kimmeridge), recalled, said he sent his two men down to Chapman's Pool in consequence of the flag signals shown by the *Treveal*. They could not be read from his station, but St Alban's was telephoned for their interpretation. He had considered the question of sending men along the coast during the night, but did not consider it necessary. He had telephoned St Alban's Head, and had been informed that a tug was going to the *Treveal*'s assistance.

Questioned by the Court as to the usual precautions taken in the case of a vessel going ashore, witness said he had dealt with a good number of cases of wreck since the war, and had always used his own discretion.

Mr Warner: Discretion was apparently not very fortunate in this case.

Witness stated that if full precautions had been taken and not been necessary it would have laid him open to censure from his superior officer. He pointed out that the volunteer life-saving company was not under his control. If he had thought the ship was standing into danger he would have put up a signal on the flagstaff and if it still came on he would have sent up a rocket or burnt a flare. He had not equipped the two men he sent to Chapman's Pool with lifelines as it would have taken 20 minutes to fetch them and the men were already heavily laden without them. He was never notified by the St Alban's coastguard that the *Treveal* had asked for a landing place. Neither did anyone even ask him for a coast patrol.

Mr Warner said that the insistence of questions relating to the coastguards' actions was not to implicate the coastguards, but had the object of finding out what precautions should be taken for saving life in the future.

FREDERICK KEELEY (Coastguard Chief Petty Officer at St Alban's

Head), recalled, said that most of the volunteer life-saving company were farm hands. It was suggested that Mr Reed, of Worth Matravers, a retired master mariner, would be able to give independent local evidence.

A Member of the Court: Did you inform in any way the men of the *Treveal* that you would patrol the coast?

Witness: No, sir. We asked if we could do anything for them, and we never got any reply to that question.

An Assessor: Would it not have been to the advantage of the crew of the ship if you had called out the volunteer company?

Witness: As things turned out it would have been advisable; but I did not think it was necessary at the time.

Witness stated that they received no notice of the wireless messages sent out by the *Treveal*. The flag signals shown by the *Treveal* in the morning were for the tug to take the crew up. Witness maintained that they were not 'distress' signals.

Mr Wilkinson pointed out that a distinction had been made between the signals the *Treveal* put up and definite distress signals which were not put up. The signals the *Treveal* put up were specific signals which had to be translated.

WILLIAM TITCOMBE (Coastguard at Kimmeridge), examined by Mr Pilcher, said he came on duty at 8 a.m. on 10 January. The weather was very dull, misty and squally. He first saw flag signals on the *Treveal* at 8.45 or 8.50 a.m., but could not read them. He rang up St Alban's Head and asked if they saw them. They answered, 'Yes, they were just reading them.' All he could hear from them was 'PYL', meaning 'I am about to abandon ship. Please keep by me to pick up my people.' Witness informed his chief officer. The chief officer instructed him to go with Petty Officer Hurden to Chapman's Pool and render any assistance they could. They left at 9.30 a.m. and arrived at Chapman's Pool at about 11.20. Witness said they took no lifelines or lifebelts, having their work cut out to get there in oilskins. When they arrived witness saw many bodies floating about in the Pool. He was informed that there were seven survivors and that Mr Piercy had gone to St Alban's Head to report. Witness went and saw the survivors at the old coastguard cottages. They were beside a fire with blankets around them. The *Treveal*'s chief engineer said, 'Are you the coastguard?' Witness replied, 'Yes,' and the chief engineer said, 'It's jolly well time you arrived.' Witness retorted that as he had had to walk about eight miles he thought he had been pretty smart. He then went to the beach to help get the bodies out. At noon 11 members of the volunteer company were at Chapman's Pool recovering bodies from the water. When witness left at 4 p.m. 15 bodies had been taken up over the cliffs.

Examined by Mr Cunliffe: He did not hear any distress rockets. If he had been sent to Chapman's Pool earlier and arrived while men were in the water he would have broken into the fishermen's huts for lines. If he had been on duty when the ship came ashore he would have sent for the lifeboat at once and informed his chief officer afterwards.

By the Court: Ordinarily it was not part of his duty to patrol the coast: 'I am simply there as a sort of glorified telephone messenger from what I can see of it.' He did not think he was on a wild goose chase to go off without lifelines and lifebelts. It would have taken 20 minutes to get them. It would have been impossible to throw a light line far against the wind, which was then blowing about 12 knots.

ARCHIBALD HURDEN (Coastguard Petty Officer at Kimmeridge), examined by Mr Pilcher, said he saw the *Treveal* on the night of 9 January. She passed the Kimmeridge station about three miles off. Visibility was very good at the time she passed and he had no doubt that the officers on the *Treveal* could see the Portland lights. Witness himself could see the lights quite plainly. He last saw the *Treveal* at 10 p.m. and did not know she was ashore until the next morning. He went with the last witness along the coast. After trying to resuscitate a man on the beach, he went on to St Alban's Head and reported to the chief officer, who, he understood, passed the message to the divisional officer. The curate also came up and spoke to the divisional officer. Witness then telephoned his own chief officer and returned to his station.

Examined by Mr Cunliffe: After the *Treveal* passed Kimmeridge station on the night of 9 January she steered a very erratic course.

GEORGE PLAIN (Coastguard Petty Officer at Swanage) said he received a message from St Alban's Head at 11 p.m. on 9 January stating that there was a steamer ashore and a tug going to her assistance. He did not think it necessary at that time to report that message to the divisional officer, who was a quarter of a mile away.

(*Mr Wilkinson* informed the court that the Admiralty had taken disciplinary action over this witness's failure to report the message to the divisional officer.)

JAMES LENNOX (Coastguard at Swanage) said he relieved the previous witness at midnight on the night of 9/10 January. Previous witness told him of the message from St Alban's Head. The telephone line to St Alban's and Kimmeridge failed between 12.30 and 5.30 a.m. At 5.30 a.m.

he managed to get a St Alban's message, via Lulworth, that the *Treveal* was hard and fast, in no immediate danger, and that the tug had not yet arrived. They often had trouble with the telephones; they were very bad.

By the Court: He knew now, but did not know at the time, that it was their duty to inform the divisional officer as soon as a vessel was reported ashore. He thought the local station officer would have taken all the necessary steps. Witness was inexperienced and had not read all the rules affecting coastguards.

(*Mr Wilkinson* informed the court that the Admiralty had also taken disciplinary action over this witness's failure to report the message to the divisional officer.)

HENRY ANDERS (Coastguard Chief Petty Officer at Lulworth), examined by Mr Pilcher, produced his signal log showing the signals which had passed through his station. The message to the Weymouth lifeboat was passed at 9.32 a.m. Another at 10.10 a.m. stated that heavy seas were breaking over the *Treveal*, and the tug could not get near enough. At 10.15 a.m. a message was passed from the secretary of the Weymouth lifeboat to the Swanage lifeboat: 'Weymouth lifeboat launched for service.' At 2.25 p.m. a message was sent from the Weymouth lifeboat stating that they had arrived at Swanage, having seen no sign of life on the *Treveal*.

(The Court adjourned for lunch.)

The scene at Chapman's Pool beach was horrendous on the morning of Saturday, 10 January: sailors' bodies gathered together, to be dragged up to the farm carts waiting at the old coastguard cottages. Going towards the sea one has a level eye view of it, but going towards the village, the journey looks daunting. On the right, the green hillside rises 350 feet, as steep as a well-roofed house. On the left, there is a deep ravine, some 150 feet to its watery floor. A dreary, dark place, grey with a covering of 'old man's beard', grey all the way to the bottom except for a few adder's berries huddled among their leaves like orange bubbles.

In the village, the building that had been bought by Captain Reed, just a few months before, for a Reading Room, was soon to be put to a macabre use: a mortuary. The violence of the hurricane had abated; the village was still. Rainwater butts overflowed, tree boughs scratched together and snowdrops, always clean and white, had broken the surface in clumps. A youth watched from a good vantage point - the village post office - as a farm cart came down Church Hill. He noticed a certain rouseabout attitude among the men on the cart and wondered why. At the corner of Pike Lane and London Row, a young girl stood and listened. She had heard the rumble of the horse and cart. The cart came into view and stopped outside the Reading Room. She saw 'their poor bones ... their poor white legs' carried inside - and she fled the scene in horror.

Charlie Newman, landlord of the Square and Compass Inn, helped the police with the task of identifying the victims of the disaster: 'In one man's wallet he found a sodden picture postcard from his children saying what a happy Christmas they had had, and that "Mum and all" would be down at the jetty to welcome him home. "It was enough to break your heart," said Charlie, "reading that, and looking down at his poor wet face steaming in the lamplight, knowing he'd never come home no more"' (Nina Warner Hooke: 'Avoidable Loss' in *Dorset*, No 70, p 11)

Late that night, a boy crept to a Reading Room window. He had seen a chink in the curtains. Peeping in he saw the sailors in sheets laid out in rows. One shrouded sailor lay in a slight draught and a curl of his hair rose and fell forlornly. The First World War's newspapers recorded the names of men killed in action; black type cluttered together like flies in a hot window. Death had lost its individuality; grief had become a mass emotion. At Worth Matravers, when carts full of dead sailors were brought to the village it was presumed that they should be buried in a mass grave. One was dug and the men laid in it - and then ordered to be taken out again. The episode is shrouded in mystery. No one knows what communications were exchanged or who was involved in the decision. The diggers of the grave were two young servicemen, Will Corben and Herbert Hooper, natives of Worth Matravers, who were home on discharge leave. Both had been involved in bringing the corpses up from Chapman's Pool. Fifty years later Will Corben could still recall the events of the weekend in detail:

"It was the worst gale that I ever saw in these parts, and I've seen plenty. More like a hurricane. Folks coming along the street had to hold on to the churchyard wall or they were knocked flat on their faces. Herbie and me went down to the Pool about midday Saturday to help fetch up the bodies. The tide was so high waves were breaking over the cliff. We tied planks together for stretchers. A hatch cover blew up the gulley and precious near killed the pair of us.

"That day we fetched up over a dozen, in a wagon from Renscombe Farm. They was three deep in the wagon. With us and all it was a fair load. Took a team of good horses to get it up to the village.

"I was on top of the heap, unloading, when a lady come by and give me a telling off for trampling on the dead. I said 'They'm past minding, missis, and so am I.'

"She didn't like that, didn't like it a bit. Come into the graveyard later on and ticked off Herbie for swearing in the presence of God. Well, by that time we'd had enough. We'd shifted a mountain of earth and banked it up against the wall while the bodies was laid in the trench. Just before the order came through to take 'em out again, the whole bloody lot fell in.

"We'd had enough. Herbie looked down at all you could see of a good ship's company under the mud and stones, most in the prime of their lives, and he said, 'If God's listening, I don't reckon he's got much to be proud of.' She didn't get much change out of Herbie and me."

(in Warner Hooke, p 15)

In contrast to the fiasco surrounding the bodies of the dead, the seven survivors were afforded every dignity, thanks to the intervention of the Shipwrecked Mariners' Society:

Just before 2 o'clock on Saturday afternoon [10 January], Mr. H. R. Lodge, the local hon. secretary ... received the news that seven men had been rescued from the wreck.

He immediately proceeded to Worth Matravers and supplied them with hot drinks and clean, dry clothing. The men were conveyed to the Anchor Hotel, Swanage.

The Shipwrecked Mariners' Society are bearing all expenses, and they are giving each man a railway ticket to proceed to his home.

(*Bournemouth Daily Echo*, 12 January 1920)

Several widows of members of the crew also came to the Anchor Hotel, to attend the inquest and personally oversee the return home of the bodies of their loved ones.

The Inquiry
Fourth Day - Monday, 10 May 1920 - Afternoon

ALFRED SPRANKLIN (Coxswain of the Weymouth Lifeboat), examined by Mr Pilcher, said that at 9.40 a.m. on 10 January he received a telegram saying that a steamer was ashore, flying distress signals. He mustered the crew and they put off at 10.07 a.m. in a moderate WSW gale. When they reached the *Treveal* they got within 100 yards to the windward of her under sail. It was then about 11.30 a.m. He did not think the weather could have been much worse. Heavy seas were breaking right over the ship and he could not see much more than her mastheads. They stood about for about three quarters of an hour but could see no sign of life on board. If they had done, he would have taken the lifeboat to the leeside of the *Treveal* and tried to get a line aboard. There would have been no difficulty in getting round to her leeside.

(He considered he could have gone alongside abreast the bridge on the leeside but did not do so on account of the danger from wreckage and as he saw no one on board. (Report of Court))

Witness said he then proceeded to Swanage, as it was impossible to get back to Weymouth.

(...the Weymouth lifeboat was forced to make for Poole Harbour. The boat on entering got on the mud off Salterns and the crew were taken off their boat by members of the Poole lifeboat crew and cared for. Later they proceeded to Weymouth by motor. The lifeboat was subsequently brought to the Ferry Steps at Poole Quay, and it will be sailed back to Weymouth by a Poole crew on the first favourable opportunity. (*Swanage Times*, 17 January 1920))

Examined by Mr Cunliffe: He was always notified of a ship ashore by the coastguards, never by Portland Dockyard. He saw the *Treveal* leave Weymouth Bay on the night of 9 January.

(Alfred Spranklin ... who was standing on Weymouth Pier when the vessel left, placed her a mile to the south of [NE $^1/_2$ E, 1 $^1/_2$ miles from the Breakwater Lighthouse]; but the position he marked on the chart differs from what he stated verbally ... [At 8.7 p.m. the Shambles light was abeam and Captain Paynter told Third Officer Donald it was two miles distant:] Alfred Spranklin ... stated she was much further off. (Report of Court))

Witness said that there were rumours in Weymouth an hour after she struck that the *Treveal* was ashore. Witness did not hear the rumours; he learnt later that there had been rumours. If he had heard the rumours on the night of 9 January he would have called out the lifeboat on his own responsibility. A tug could have towed him within a quarter of a mile, south, east or west of the *Treveal*. If he had wanted a tug he would have had to apply to the Admiralty by ringing up Portland Dockyard. Witness stated that he had often been over the Kimmeridge Ledge. If a vessel was left on the Ledge for more than one tide in bad weather it was all up with her. Witness was of opinion that the tug *Pilot* could not have got alongside the *Treveal* in such a nasty gale as was blowing on the morning of 10 January. In such weather there was no chance of successfully beaching a ship's boat in Chapman's Pool without local knowledge. If witness had taken the crew of the *Treveal* off he would have beached his boat on the east side of Chapman's Pool, towards St Alban's Head. He would regard any vessel on Kimmeridge Ledge as being in danger, and the lives of the crew in danger in rough weather. *By the Court*: If he had got to the wreck during the night he could have taken the crew off. At the wreck in the morning he saw her funnel washed away and a big rent in her starboard side. He did not see the tug *Pilot* at all and thought the crew of the *Treveal* must have left in their boats, been picked up by the tug and proceeded to Swanage.

ALBERT MASTERS (Formerly Acting Secretary of the Weymouth Lifeboat) said that in his experience any vessel on the Kimmeridge Ledge was in great danger. If he had had information from St Alban's Head that the ship was ashore, he would have sent out the lifeboat.

HAROLD INNES (District Inspector of the National Lifeboat Institution) said that they usually received their information of casualties from the coastguards, they being the coast watchers, but the coxswain had authority to turn the lifeboat out on receiving information from anyone. As a matter of fact lifeboats were often launched on hearsay when there was no ship aground at all. It was part of the duty of coastguards to inform them of any casualty. It was not part of the duty of the police, though they often did receive information from them. The Weymouth lifeboat was in a perfectly seaworthy condition and as regards the crew uniformly good reports had been given.

WILLIAM HAYSOM (Secretary of the Swanage Lifeboat) said he first heard of the wreck at 10.45 a.m. on 10 January and received a message that the Weymouth lifeboat had been launched for service. He sent a message to ask whether the Swanage lifeboat was required, and the answer from St Alban's Head was that it was not. Any time up to 8 a.m. on 10 January, before the wind got up so rough, the Swanage lifeboat could have got round the Head, if witness had been notified.

HENRY BURDEN (Secretary of the Poole Lifeboat) said his boat was not called out. He knew nothing of the wreck until the Weymouth lifeboat came into Poole Harbour at 8 p.m. on the following day. He said he had carried out salvage operations in the vicinity of the wreck and said the coast near Chapman's Pool was very dangerous and strewn with large boulders. He did not know any part of the coast between Weymouth and the Isle of Wight so dangerous as the coastline along by St Alban's Head. He said the *Treveal*'s boats had no earthly chance in Chapman's Pool, and he considered it very unwise on the part of the crew that they should have ever left the ship. (Witness submitted photographs of two vessels previously aground on the Kimmeridge Ledge.) He said that any vessel on the Ledge was in danger from the time she struck, and the lives of the crew unquestionably.

CHARLES COOMBES (Manager of Messrs G H Collins & Co, Portland), examined by Mr Pilcher, said that at about 10 p.m. on 9 January he received a telephone message from the Harbourmaster's office, Portland Dockyard, informing him that a wireless message had been received by Rame Head from the *Treveal*, stating that she was aground and asking for a tug. Unfortunately, Collins & Co's own tug, *Petrel*, was in Weymouth undergoing repairs, but, as this was known to the Dockyard authorities, witness asked if the Government tug *Pilot* might be sent. The request was granted. There were no other tugs at Portland. There were no tugs at Weymouth under steam: it would have taken 10 or 12 hours to get up steam. Next morning, the *Petrel*'s repairs having been finished, she was sent out at 10 a.m., with instructions to stand by the lifeboat and render all assistance possible.

By the Court: It did not occur to him when he received the first message to communicate with the lifeboat. His attention was directed to getting the ship off.

WILLIAM TORRANCE (Master of the *St Keverne*) said he did not notice the course the *Treveal* took when she left Portland.

(William Torrance ... who brought letters to the *Treveal* just before she proceeded, left Portland Harbour by the North Entrance to close the ship, which he states was lying in a position NE $1/2$ E, 1 $1/2$ miles from the Breakwater Lighthouse. (Report of Court))

(The Court adjourned.)

News of the loss of the *Treveal* began to circulate in St Ives on Saturday. Captain Kemp recalled:

> That night, Saturday night, I was going - my father had a barber's

shop on the Wharf, had it for years - and I was coming home from
there, and I was only 14, and I met a survivor's brother that
evening, a fellow called Curnow, a road-sweeper. His brother
was a messroom boy in the *Treveal*, and he was running up the
street and he had just heard by one of the fishermen that the
Treveal was lost outside of Portland, and his brother was in it, and
he was nearly demented, and he was going home then to see his
mother. I can remember quite well it was an awful night, a
Saturday night, and it was blowing a sou'west gale.

It was another day before Charles Argall, at Truro, brother of the
Treveal apprentice Frederick Argall, learnt of the disaster. He recalled:
'When I left school I entered Truro post office as a sorter, and I was doing
the morning mail ... The newspapers were there and you weren't
supposed to take the wrappers off but I saw something and I opened the
wrapper and there I read that the *Treveal* had sunk, with seven survivors,
including Frederick Argall ... That was the first information I got of it -
the first information the family got of it.'

Most families, of course, did not experience relief, but grief. Mrs
Brassington, Captain Paynter's niece, remembered as a child opening
the door on a dark evening to a Hain official who had come to break the
news personally. In other cases a telegram brought the news, which, in
the case of Peter Cogar's family, was followed speedily by a letter from
the Secretary of the Hain company:

Dear Cousin,
S. S. "TREVEAL".
You will have received our telegrams saying that poor Peter's
body has been identified and we have also arranged for same to
be brought here for burial. The wires are down so that it may be
some little time before you receive same.
You must arrange a conveyance somehow to Helston Station
and in case of need if there is no cab or anything at St. Keverne,
telegraph to Helston for a motor for yourself and the girls.
I will let you have all particulars when you come down.
Yours very Sincerely,
William Cogar.

Chapter 8

I had finally spoken to Malcolm Donald, son of the *Treveal*'s third officer, on the telephone, and was walking down to the Square and Compass Inn to mull over what he had said. I took a detour into the Worth Matravers churchyard and made my way to the top of the north side, the 'unlucky' side, traditionally the burial place of the unbaptised. Backed by a long, low mound - a trace of the mass grave that had been dug for the crew of the *Treveal* - stood the headstone for the two crewmen who were, eventually, buried at Worth Matravers. The stone is inscribed -

HERE LIE
THE UNIDENTIFIED BODIES OF
TWO MEMBERS OF THE CREW OF
S.S. TREVEAL DROWNED ON
JANUARY 10TH 1920
WHEN THEIR SHIP WAS WRECKED
OFF ST ALBAN'S HEAD
WITH THE LOSS OF 36 LIVES.

I walked back down the hill and paused to read the inscriptions on several other stones. Andrew Cory Reed, died 1919, aged 84 years. Clerk of the Woolwich Local Board of Health for 45 years. Edith Emily Reed, daughter of Andrew Cory and Jemima Reed. Captain Edward Reed, son of the same, formerly of the Merchant Navy, died 24 April 1947, aged 81 years: 'Benefactor of this village'.

Captain Reed was a prominent figure at Worth Matravers at the time of the *Treveal* disaster and was foreman of the jury at the coroner's inquests. His finger had been very active at the auction sale of the village the previous year and thereafter he provided some villagers with cottages to rent; gardens for others; a withy bed for the fishermen to make their pots; a Reading Room, complete with every sort of game; even fireworks on 5 November. He looked every inch a village squire, with his red jowls and flowing white hair; and he is remembered as a patriarchal figure.

Today, the Reed family grave is overgrown with tangled grass, nettles and seeding docks - as is the grave adjacent to it, with its headstone in memory of Emily Barnes, who died on 19 September 1910, aged 63.

Most gravestones seem to 'know' each other: they are huddled together in convivial groups. Thus, to find a stone out of place - so to speak - begs an explanation. Captain Reed, from around the turn of the century, lived with his sister Edith in a house overlooking the Channel. In a little cottage behind their home lived Emily Barnes, a recluse of whom nothing was known. Captain Reed always said he would never marry, unless to 'a lady', and he never did. Gossip, however, connected him and Miss Barnes to the extent that a story circulated that a first mate's uniform had been seen in a trunk in her cottage, which, in turn, added fuel to the rumour that Edward Reed never was a captain.

To get to the bottom of the question I had applied to the National Maritime Museum for his certificates of competency. It emerged that he had passed his examination for a master's certificate in 1893 - although he never went to sea in that capacity. Maybe he wanted to become captain to, as Ruskin said, be called captain. Yet this cut no ice with the fishermen of Worth Matravers. The men who gathered outside his house and along his wall - the Pond Head Parliament - were certainly not respectful of his rank, if, as they questioned, rank he had. This sort of doubt was once quite common. In Thomas Hardy's *Return of the Native* Mrs Yeobright says of Captain Vye, 'They call him captain, but anybody is captain'; and later, 'No doubt he has been to sea in some tub or other.'

Eddie Reed's father, Andrew Cory Reed, was an invalid and used to sit at an upper window with his telescope, watching vessels going up and down Channel - maybe verifying his son's observations, maybe chuckling, for the 'locals' would often argue about the type of ship crossing the bay.

'Square-rigger coming up, Mr Reed.'

'No, no, its a brigantine.'

''Tis a square-rigger if ever I saw one.'

An argument would rumble on, Eddie continuing over the sniggering, because he never knew how much was 'bait', or whether they really thought him 'fishy'.

But there was one topic on which they all seemed agreed: the menace of education. Captain Reed said that it would be the ruination of the country. Even Amos Bower, the Worth farm labourer who was sacked at the end of each week for insolence, agreed with the sentiment: ''Twill be the ruination of the country all right - 'taint bloody natural for people like we.' The Reading Room was run by Captain Reed with the aim of instilling the rudiments of King, Country, Empire and Good Citizenship, before the pressures of the Square and Compass taught their sorrows to swim. The room was very well-equipped: playing cards, darts, dominoes, draughts and a shooting gallery. Reading Room was a misnomer. There was no reading matter there of any kind.

With education safely out of the way, the law came strongly into its own. Frank Lander had to pay Captain Reed a shilling a year to cross a few inches of the captain's land which stood between the Landers' cottage and their outside privy - because 'it was the law'. Dirty work preceded Captain Reed's purchase of Edwin Bower's cottage at the village sale in 1919; exactly how dirty no one knew. But thereafter the captain was very generous to Edwin, and his son, Buff; and when, later, the captain was on his deathbed, it was Mrs Edwin, as she was called, who he asked to nurse him. One day, after he had 'been away' (for an operation which only delayed his death a while longer), the wild belle of the village rushed up to him and he turned his head aside with the words 'Don't kiss me'. From being a regular non-churchgoer he took squire's seat, right up for'ad and never missed a service. On a spring day, the benefactor, the captain, the self-styled squire died, of cancer of the lip - and despite his oft-professed deference to the law, left his affairs in a terrible mess.

When Eddie Reed died, he took with him - to the bottom as it were - the ethos, myth and fantasia of village life up to that time. Reed's House, as his stone cottage was known, was bought by a gravel merchant from Christchurch and re-named Gulliver's Cottage, after the famous smuggler - romantic nonsense as far as Worth Matravers people were concerned, who knew smuggling as a serious and dangerous trade. Their ancient connections with it were not put on show. Hidy-holes had been plastered over, lobster pots could not speak and dark ancestral deeds were whispered of as if informants and Revenue men might still be eavesdropping. Worth Matravers people had felt great sympathy for a maid at Weston Farm, whose 'young man' was shot and killed by Revenue men at Seacombe, and their descendents still felt the past too keenly to make light of it.

Smuggling was not the only trade which enabled a poor Purbeck man to supplement his income in former times: 'Thomas Bond told an antiquarian meeting at Corfe Castle in March 1867: "The Purbeck peasants appear to have been no less addicted to the lawless practice of wrecking than were ... the inhabitants of other sea coasts ... "' (Rodney Legg: *Purbeck Island*, p 63). Although the *Treveal's* course from Portland could hardly have been better plotted by a wrecker, those days had long since passed. The practice may, however, have been the root of a country game played in the era of the *Treveal*. It was called 'Dicky Dyke show you light' and was winter entertainment. A lad would set off, often along the seashore, with a covered lantern. After quarter of an hour he would remove the lantern's guard and hold up the light. He was then chased to wherever they thought he was. If he was too long before 'showing', they would all shout 'Dicky Dyke show your light'. In the twentieth century, Purbeck people no longer bore sailors any ill will. One preacher at Worth Matravers took a ship on the sea as a kind of sea sand timer. If, when he began his sermon, a ship was crossing Winspit Bay in one window and, in the fullness of time, appeared in the next, then his sermon had gone on too long. One member of the congregation, the organist, once said she didn't mind how long a preacher's sermon went on for because she thought the large lamplit windows might help sailors at sea.

Following the *Treveal* disaster there was widespread sympathy among the people of Purbeck. One of the St Ives newspapers reported: 'Mr. C. E. West, Clerk to the Swanage Urban District Council, has addressed the following letter to the Town Clerk of St. Ives (Mr. Edward Boase):- "At a meeting of this Council, held last night, I was instructed to write expressing my Council's sympathy with the relatives of those so unhappily lost in the Treveal. I understand that many of the crew were inhabitants of St. Ives"' (*Western Echo*, 17 January 1920).

However, beneath the universal mourning lay different nuances of belief - exemplified by the rumours which sprang up at the different places in the immediate aftermath of the disaster.

At Worth Matravers it was said that the captain of the *Treveal* had *refused* to take a pilot on board at Portland. It was also said that he had got ashore and was 'making for the Continent' - the obvious implication being that he had something to hide; that he was in some way 'guilty'. An old man, long dead, who had lived at Langton Matravers, told me that when he heard of the disaster he decided to walk to Chapman's Pool to see the wreck. He walked via Gallows Gore through Coombe Bottom. ''Twas getting dark,' he said. Passing some tall scrub, he 'looked up and saw a man, motionless, in black uniform ...' He turned and ran, not stopping until he reached the street of Langton Matravers.

At St Ives, altogether different rumours circulated. In my interview with Captain Kemp, he had recalled one which was prevalent at the time: 'They said that the captain might've come out of the chart room and shouted up the course to steer out of Portland and in the wind, with

Charlie Paynter being a St Ives man and the third officer being a Welshman, the different dialects ...' Another rumour which circulated at St Ives was that vital wireless messages from the *Treveal*, which might have changed the whole course of events, were jammed by Portland warships.

The rumours were, as later emerged, just rumours, but they are potent in demonstrating how, from the outset, the two communities sought to affix blame away from their respective selves.

Meanwhile, the extent of the *Treveal* disaster was being highlighted in the press with each passing day. The body of Joseph Kavanagh, one of the wireless operators, was recovered from the Solent and 'The body of another sailor, also believed to be a victim of the wreck of the Treveal was washed ashore at Brooke, Isle of Wight ... On the left forearm is tattooed the figure of a woman wearing a sailor's jumper and straw hat' (*St Ives Times*, 30 January 1920).

The Inquiry
Fifth Day - Tuesday, 11 May 1920 - Morning

EDWARD REED (Retired Master Mariner, residing at Worth Matravers, and a member of the Volunteer Life-Saving Company) said he heard no distress rockets on the morning of 10 January. He had some experience in Norway as to the echo of steamers' whistles from high cliffs, and he thought it was quite possible that the sound of the rockets had been thrown back to sea from the cliffs and consequently not heard at St Alban's Head. Witness stated that the volunteer company were an energetic lot and would not have complained had they been called out on a wild goose chase. He had never known a man absent when the company was called out. They were always paid on such occasions, even if not made use of.

(JOHN SMITH WRIGHT (Coastguard Divisional Officer, stationed at Swanage) interpolated that from his own knowledge the volunteer company were a very enthusiastic and able body of men.)

CHARLES NEWMAN (Landlord of the Square and Compass Inn at Worth Matravers, and captain of the Volunteer Life-Saving Company), examined by Mr Pilcher, said the company was usually called out by the coastguards by means of a rocket signal. Witness would wait for instructions from the coastguards unless he was sure their services were required. He stated that the rocket cart had never been to Chapman's Pool. It could not get further than the old coastguard cottages. He said that on the morning of 10 January he heard some sounds but thought it

The Worth Matravers 'Rocket Crew' (mid-1920s)

Those present include: Sid Lander (standing, back row, far right); Miller Lander (kneeling, middle row, second from right); Amos Bower (kneeling, middle row, far right); Charlie Newman (sitting, front row, far left); and William Bower (sitting, front row, second from right).

was the Tank Corps at gun practice at Bovington Camp. He was not informed there was a ship ashore and the first he heard was that there were bodies floating in Chapman's Pool. He went down at once and got there about noon. Mr Hurden, the Kimmeridge coastguard, was there then.

Examined by Mr Cunliffe: He had been captain of the volunteer company for 11 years. He could not recall a previous occasion when his company had not been called out when a vessel came ashore. The men were always ready to turn out when wanted, day or night. There were plenty of lines in the fishermen's huts, about 100 yards from the Pool. He would defy the world to throw lines out against the wind on 10 January. It was blowing right into Chapman's Pool. The waves, he thought, were 'upwards of 30 feet.'

Mr Cunliffe: Would a telephone apparatus to your house facilitate matters in calling the company out?

Witness: That is exactly what is required, and always was, sir.

By the Court: Even if the rocket apparatus had been got down to Chapman's Pool, if the rocket had been fired over the upturned boats it would have cut two or three men off the boat. He did not think he would have taken the risk. He could only have waited to see if the sea washed the men to the shore and then pulled them out the same as Mr Piercy and Mr Lander did. He did not think anyone could have swum out with a line round his waist. The general feeling of the volunteer company was that if they had been called out to Chapman's Pool they would not have been much help, but if the *Treveal*'s boats had gone to Pier Bottom the rocket apparatus could have been used there.

WILLIAM BOWER (Quarryman, of Winspit, and a member of the Volunteer Life-Saving Company) said he got down to Chapman's Pool at about 1 p.m. on 10 January, and helped to bring up the bodies. He said they generally heard the rocket signal but he thought a telephone would be a great help. He agreed with Mr Newman that if the volunteer company had been called out to Chapman's Pool they could not have done much to help.

I wandered out of the churchyard and up to the Square and Compass Inn. There is no better panoramic view of Worth Matravers and its environs than from the 'sitting wall' outside the inn. While Pond Head (Captain Reed's steps) was the lower house of the village Parliament, the 'Square' was its House of Lords. They came from far and wide: legal and theatre people, writers and artists ... sitting with the village regulars.

The landlord, Charlie Newman, with his fund of local yarns, his knowledge of a good each-way bet, his shuffle and his chuckle, presided over a place apart set on a hill. It was home to the Ancient Order of Purbeck Marblers and Stonecutters, who used the inn each year, on 2 February, for its 'Kissing Day' feast. Estate cottage rents were paid here and weightier village concerns voiced.

Charlie Newman was a regular churchgoer, who shared the front pew with Eddie Reed (after Eddie had taken up churchgoing), one at either side at Morning Service. Charlie was a natty dresser. He usually wore a well-cut brown suit to church and, in summer, a red-rose button-hole; he had an eye for a pretty thing. The organist, Floss Welsh, slowed the hymns and responses almost to a drawl - more Te deum laudanum than laudamus - and the congregation swayed like drunks.

Today, another Charlie Newman, the fourth generation to pull pints at the Square, maintains the family tradition of having something up his sleeve. How many pubs in Dorset can boast a landlord who is also an antiquarian and curator of a fine museum? At the Square and Compass you can sit in the shiny-walled tap room on a rough bench, in front of a blazing log fire, and feel forever rescued.

I took out the notes of my telephone conversation with Malcolm Donald and wrote them up:

Q. You said in your letter that there are stories to do with the sinking of the *Treveal* which have passed down through your family?

A. There are one or two things, but of course I wasn't around at the time and Daddy died in tragic circumstances in I think 1936, unfortunately, and I was only about five years old then.

Q. What were the things you heard about the *Treveal*?

A. Well, we have a Bible which Mum always said, 'That's what Daddy came out of the water with.'

Q. Really ...

A. That was when they abandoned ship.

Q. Was that his own Bible do you suppose, or perhaps the ship's - is there any inscription or writing in it?

A. No, no writing at all.

Q. And you say he had this Bible with him when he came out of Chapman's Pool?

A. That's what I've always been told. It looks like it's been in contact with water at some time.

Q. That's remarkable that he had it with him - that he went to that trouble and must have had it wrapped in oilskin or something waterproof, and that he managed to hang on to it in a terrible sea ...

A. Yes, and he was pulled out of Chapman's Pool by his hair, and that was by your grandfather of course, and his hair stood on end for week's afterwards.

Q. Stood on end -

A. For weeks afterwards.

Q. And my grandfather's hair turned white almost overnight ...

A. It must have been a terrible experience with only, what was it, a fifth of the crew survived.

Q. Was your father always with the Hain company afterwards?

A. No, he became a pilot later, here, at Swansea.

Q A pilot?

A. Yes.

Q. That's interesting ... Did you hear anything else about the *Treveal*? Did you ever hear anything about Captain Paynter?

A. Paynter, no.

Q. And you don't remember hearing anything else about the *Treveal*?

A. No, nothing.

Q. Nothing at all?

A. My elder sister may know something. I could ask her. She's two or three years older than me. She may remember something ...

I went to the bar for another pint and sat back down. I wondered if it would be worth going to Swansea to talk to Malcolm Donald face-to-face. It was interesting that his father had become a pilot of all things. The question had been put to William Donald, in the very room in which I was then sitting, if he thought the catastrophe would have happened if there had been a pilot on board the *Treveal*. The Coroner had not allowed the question to be answered. Was Donald's later career an answer to that question?

An inquest on 20 members of the crew of the SS *Treveal* was held at the Square and Compass Inn, on Monday, 12 January 1920, before Mr Maddock, Deputy Coroner for East Dorset, and a jury. The Foreman of the jury was Mr E R J Reed, retired master mariner.

Captain F Uren, marine superintendent, represented the Hain Steamship Company; Mr G Coombes, of Portland, represented Messrs Collins & Co, the ship's agents; Mr W Wilkinson, Admiralty law agent, of Weymouth, represented the Admiralty; and Supt H Toop, of Wareham, represented the Dorset County Police.

The scope of the inquest was far more limited than that of the later

Board of Trade inquiry. William Donald gave evidence. Frederick Burt and Ernest Burt (respectively senior pilot, Portland, and master of the tug *Pilot*) gave evidence. Coastguard Chape and Petty Officer Scullard of St Alban's Head gave evidence. The Reverend Horace Piercy gave evidence and 'the fisherman Lander corroborated'. The Coroner, at times, found it hard to hide his exasperation, particularly during the evidence of Petty Officer Scullard, complaining at one point: 'There is so much waiting about for somebody else to come. That is what I cannot understand. What I have not yet made out is why nobody troubled to go down any nearer.' He had regained his composure by the close of the inquest:

> THE CORONER said the occurrence was a matter for the deepest regret. He had been asked by the steamship company to express their deepest sorrow and sympathy to the relatives and friends. It was clear that up to about 9 a.m. on Saturday the captain and the crew had every hope that the ship would last out, and they would be taken off as soon as the tug could come within range. They went through a terrible night. When the weather worsened and began to smash the boats and threatened to break up the ship, the captain's judgment to abandon ship was justified. The coastguards were not quite clear about hearing some of the signals. The captain of the tug had to consider the 20 lives immediately in his charge. Nothing occurred at the coastguard station to make them think it was a case of urgent necessity until about 8.40 a.m., Saturday, and they had no reason to get the life-saving apparatus out. But he could not help thinking, and perhaps the authorities might consider it for the future, that the life-saving apparatus crew have been called together on the chance of saving life. There was a good deal of waiting for one another, but perhaps that was natural.
>
> THE JURY returned a verdict of 'Accidentally drowned through the foundering of the vessel.' They suggested that telephonic communication be established between the village of Worth Matravers and St Alban's Head coastguard station.
>
> THE CORONER, at the request of Captain Uren, thanked the Reverend Piercy and Mr Lander for their gallant assistance in helping to rescue the survivors, and the two young ladies who helped to restore the rescued were also thanked.

Later in the week, Mr Maddock, in holding a further inquest at Worth Matravers regarding the finding of one of the bodies of the crew of the *Treveal*, announced that he had summoned a jury again in the hope that points which had arisen and which did not appear clear might be cleared up.

The only witness reported to have given evidence at the second inquest was Frederick Keeley, the station officer at St Alban's Head coastguard station. Why Keeley did not give evidence at the first inquest is not known. As with Petty Officer Scullard on the previous occasion, the Coroner became somewhat exasperated by Chief Petty Officer Keeley:

The Coroner: Anybody leaving the vessel would presumably make for Chapman's Pool, so that, although they signalled that they were leaving the ship something before 9 o'clock, you did not send any men down where they would be most likely to land, did you?

Witness: I understood by the signals that the tug was coming near. We had men to watch to see if boats left the ship, and what direction they made for.

The Coroner: Did it occur to you that it would be advisable to send down to the place where the men would obviously come to land?

Witness: I did not know that the crew were going to land.

Again, by the close of the inquest the Coroner had regained his equanimity:

THE CORONER, reviewing the evidence, said he could not suggest that there had been any actual negligence. Everybody concerned - those on board the ship and those on shore - undoubtedly were under the impression that all the men on the ship were in a state more or less of security until 7.30 to 8 o'clock on the Saturday morning. Still, it was a pity arrangements were not made at Chapman's Pool for what actually happened.

THE JURY returned a verdict similar to that returned at the earlier inquest, recommending that telephonic communication should be established between the village of Worth Matravers and the coastguard station, and that a lifebelt station should be maintained at Chapman's Pool.

JOHN SMITH WRIGHT, Coastguard Divisional Officer, stationed

at Swanage, said such a station could be easily established, and he would bring the matter to the notice of the Board of Trade. St Alban's coastguard station was to be rebuilt this year on another site, and he would ask the Board to move the life-saving apparatus there. The apparatus was practically useless in its present position. THE CORONER, on behalf of Captain Uren, marine superintendent, expressed the sincere sympathy of the Hain Steamship Company with the relatives of the men who had lost their lives. The company, observed the Coroner, had done all in their power to help the relatives in the sad offices of getting their dead ones home for burial.

The inquests fanned the flames of rumour and debate - as did Captain Uren's continuing inability to board the *Treveal* and search for any documents which might explain how the ship had gone aground.

Visibility was good in Weymouth Bay on Monday [12 January], and it was seen that the steamer Treveal was in two portions, 80 feet apart.
    She is perfectly upright, her bow points to the rocks she struck, and the stern has slewed round towards the shore at an angle of 45 degrees. (*Western Echo*, 17 January 1920)

Lloyd's Agent at Weymouth reported on Tuesday [13 January]:- "Weather unfit to attempt to board the Treveal. Viewed the vessel from the cliffs. To all appearance both portions are rapidly breaking up. No 3 bulkhead and some 20 feet shell plating after end, forward body, torn away since yesterday. After body settling down. Considerable quantity jute washing ashore, mixed with seaweed. Recommend making the best arrangements possible with a local contractor, and endeavour to salve the cargo now washing ashore and any fittings." (*St Ives Times*, 16 January 1920)

The biggest debate immediately after the disaster was that which centred around the question which the Coroner had ruled Third Officer Donald could not answer: would the catastrophe have occurred if there had been a pilot aboard the *Treveal*? At the later Board of Trade inquiry this question was never really discussed, the court having decided - once it was established that the *Treveal* called at Portland for a *North Sea* pilot - that: 'This fact had nothing to do with the casualty, as the pilot was required to assist the master in the navigation of the North Sea and on to Dundee' (Report of Court). But in the immediate aftermath feeling had run high on whether or not the lack of a pilot was to blame for the loss of the *Treveal*. 'THE PILOT QUESTION', as one newspaper (*Southern Times*, 17 January 1920) termed it, was endlessly discussed.

At the Board of Trade inquiry the following exchange would take place between the Court and Hains' managing director, Robert Sawle Read:

A Member of the Court: Did the captain try and get a pilot at Portland?
Witness: Yes.
The Member of the Court: He did not get one?
Witness: No.
(A telegram was produced which was dispatched to the Hain company from Messrs Collins & Co (agents) Portland, stating that the *Treveal* had called at Portland for a North Sea pilot, but proceeded, as no pilot was awaiting her.)
The President: Was there no local pilot?
Witness: They wanted a North Sea pilot in connection with the mines.

On the face of it, Mr Read's evidence, which suggests that decisions about pilots were the responsibility of the captain, does not sit altogether comfortably alongside the statement, already mentioned, which appeared in one of the first press reports following the disaster (*Western Morning News*, 12 January 1920): that when no pilot was available at Portland, Hains' agents '*instructed* Capt. Paynter to proceed without one ...' (My emphasis.)

So, who made the decision to proceed? There is a scenario which largely reconciles Mr Read's evidence with what was stated in the press: namely, that Captain Paynter possessed the discretion which Mr Read said he did, but rather than exercising it, when faced with the situation at Portland, preferred to seek company guidance as to what course of action to adopt; and was instructed to proceed. This scenario not only reconciles the apparent contradiction between the evidence of Mr Read and the statement in the *Western Morning News*, but it is entirely consistent with what is known about the type of man Captain Paynter was.

If the foregoing accounts for one aspect of 'THE PILOT QUESTION', a new problem arises from an attempt by the *Southern Times* (17 January 1920) to resolve another aspect:

> Some misconception appears to have arisen locally in regard to the question of a pilot not being provided the Treveal. The whole of the facts do not appear to have come out at the inquest. What happened was that the Treveal put into Portland on Friday evening for a Dundee pilot, the vessel being instructed at the Suez Canal to call here. In this case no pilot was sent down, which is not unusual, as of course is well known in shipping circles. Portland is simply used as a convenient port of call to pick up a pilot and if one has not been sent the vessel goes out again. *Had the Treveal applied for a local pilot she could, of course, have had one; but in that case a local pilot would only have seen her clear of the Breakwater, and headed her on her course.* (My emphasis.)

In other words, aside from the North Sea pilot, the *Treveal* could have taken a local pilot if she had wished - and doubtless it was this fact which led to the Worth Matravers rumour that Captain Paynter had *refused* a pilot. On this point there are two things to say. First, the *Southern Times* seems to have been under the impression that the *Treveal* went *into* Portland Harbour, for the paragraph envisages a local pilot seeing the ship 'clear of the Breakwater'; second, pilot or no pilot, Captain Paynter should have been perfectly capable of charting a safe course. As Captain Kemp had said when I interviewed him at St Ives: 'The captain is always in charge of his ship, and the pilot is only there to *assist* the master. The pilot can come aboard and sit on a chair and tell the master what to do to get out of shallow water say, but he's only there to *assist* the master in the navigation of the ship ... You're blamed whether you have a pilot or not.'

The Inquiry
Fifth Day - Tuesday, 11 May 1920 - Morning (continued)

EDWIN REID (Chief Petty Officer of the Admiralty wireless station at Culver Cliff, Isle of Wight), examined by Mr Pilcher, produced extracts from the station's log, of messages affecting the *Treveal* on the night of 9/10 January. At 11.49 p.m. the *Treveal* called witness's station and stated that they had a priority message. His station consequently asked all ships to cease transmitting. At 11.52 p.m. the *Treveal* called 'Urgent' but the message was jammed. At 11.54 p.m. all ships were again asked to cease transmitting, and he asked the *Treveal* to repeat her message, but the United States ship *Irving* was still working and had to be called again. At 12.01 a.m. the *Treveal* was again jammed but from an unknown source came: '*Treveal* wants assistance at once.' At 12.04 a.m. his station acknowledged a message from the *Treveal*: 'Radio Urgent to Hain St Ives. *Treveal* ashore St Alban's Head. Water in three holds and flooding engine room. Paynter.' This message was forwarded by land wire through Portsmouth. At 5.25 a.m. his station received another urgent message for the owners from the *Treveal*: 'Radio No 1 to Hain, St Ives, Cornwall. Nos 1, 2, 3 and 4 tanks and bilges full. Send salvage steamer and lighter. Paynter.' This message was forwarded by land wire through Portsmouth. At 7.05 a.m. the *Treveal* sent a further message to witness's station: 'Radio No 3 Steamship *Treveal* to Brocklebank Line, Liverpool. *Treveal* ashore St Alban's Head.' This message was also forwarded by land wire through Portsmouth. At 7.56 a.m. the *Treveal* sent out a message to all ships: 'SOS. SOS. SOS. *Treveal* now abandoning ship. Ship breaking up quickly. Taking to boats off St Alban's Head. Surely hurry.' Witness's station passed this message to the Commander-in-Chief at Portsmouth and to 'All ships'. Witness stated that at 7.57 a.m. the SS *Matiba* called the *Treveal* and asked her 'What is your position?' The *Treveal* replied: 'Here, ashore. SOS. SOS. Taking to boats.' That was the last message from the *Treveal* witness's station received.

By the Court: His station received no message reading 'For God's sake send assistance.'

HENRY WOOLLACOMBE (Lieutenant, HMS *Orion*), examined by Mr Pilcher, produced extracts from a signal log, of messages affecting the *Treveal* received and sent by his ship on the night of 9/10 January. The first was, 'Urgent. G H Collins, Portland. Send tug boat to St Alban's Head. *Treveal* ashore,' which was passed to witness's ship by HMS *Gibraltar* at 10 p.m. The log stated that this message was passed to the King's Harbourmaster, Portland, who had ordered a tug, *Pilot*, to proceed to St Alban's Head as soon as the crew was mustered. Witness said that at 12.20 a.m. his ship sent to the *Treveal*, 'Tug leaving Portland for your assistance' and at 12.26 a.m. they received a message from the *Treveal*, via HMS *Monarch*, 'Water is now two feet from dynamo. SOS. Hurry.' At 12.59 a.m. witness's ship received a message from the *Treveal* to 'Any British Warship' timed at 12.47 a.m., 'Have tugs wireless please?' At 1.34 a.m. witness's ship sent to the *Treveal*: 'Your 00.47. Tug *Pilot* not fitted with wireless. Should arrive shortly.' At 2.47 a.m. witness's ship received from the *Treveal*, 'Have you anything to communicate. Tug not yet arrived,' and at 3.02 a.m. witness's ship replied, 'When tug arrives communicate with her by flashing.' Witness's ship first received the *Treveal*'s triple SOS message at 8.15 a.m.

EDWARD DOWNING (Signal Boatswain of HMS *Gibraltar*), examined by Mr Pilcher, produced his ship's signal log and read the messages received and sent out on the night of 9/10 January. His ship received the *Treveal*'s message 'Urgent. G H Collins, Portland. Send tug boat to St Alban's Head. *Treveal* ashore' at 9.51 p.m. His ship received 'SOS. Steamship *Treveal* ashore St Alban's Head,' at 10.45 p.m. and 'SNO Portland. Steamer ashore St Alban's Head. Requires tugs immediately,' at 10.56 p.m. Further entries in witness's signal log corroborated the evidence of the previous witnesses.

(A record of messages received by Rame Head, certified by the Admiral commanding coastguard, was also put before the Court.)

On the morning of Thursday, 15 January, the two St Ives survivors of the *Treveal* disaster - Allan Woolcock and Thomas Curnow - arrived home by train. Later the same day four of the five recovered bodies of St Ives victims also arrived home. The *St Ives Times* (16 January 1920) reported:

The 4.43 p.m. train yesterday brought four of the St. Ives victims home for interment, the sorrowful home-coming being witnessed by a large number of bereaved relatives and sympathising friends, who lined the Malakoff, the Terrace, railway station and its precincts.

The onlookers stood reverently, with uncovered heads, while the bodies were tenderly removed from the van in which they had been conveyed from the scene of the disaster, to the hearses in waiting to receive them.

The train brought all that remained immortal of Garfield Andrews (assistant steward), P. Cogar (carpenter), H. Pearce (A.B.) and W. Phillips (assistant cook), all of whom left St. Ives about three months ago full of strength and vigour, to carry out their respective duties on board the s.s. Treveal. They were all removed to their late respective homes.

The body of J. Bassett, who was picked up on Wednesday evening is expected to arrive at St. Ives to-day (Friday) or tomorrow ...

No information of the recovery of the bodies of Capt. Paynter and T. Noall has yet been received.

The first two funerals, those of Peter Cogar and Henry Pearce, took place on Friday, 16 January.

The body of Peter Cogar was taken into the Primitive Methodist Chapel, where a service was conducted by the Reverend J G Cushing, who was accompanied on the rostrum by the Mayor of St Ives, Mr J Daniel, junior. Among the mourners were Peter's widow, Mary, and his cousin, William, Secretary of the Hain company. William Cogar also represented Robert Sawle Read, who was unavoidably detained in London. The interment at Barnoon Cemetery was witnessed by the *Treveal* survivor Allan Woolcock.

A large procession of relatives and friends, the latter chiefly seafaring men, attended the funeral of Henry Pearce. The coffin was taken to the cemetery from his home at North Place. The service was conducted by the Reverend W F Charlton (United Methodist), and among those present was the Mayor of St Ives. Henry's widow was unable to attend, being prevented by indisposition from travelling from Liverpool.

The funeral of William Phillips took place the following day, Saturday, and was attended by his sorrowing parents, with a large gathering of relatives and sympathising townspeople. About 40 ex-servicemen, in command of Captain T Uren, were present. The corpse was borne from his home to the Salvation Army Hall, the mournful cortege being headed by the Salvation Army band, playing the Dead March. At the conclusion of the preliminary service at the hall, the solemn cortege was reformed, and wended its way to the cemetery.

The last two funerals, those of Garfield Andrews and James Bassett, took place on Sunday.

The Reverend Cushing (Primitive Methodist) officiated at the funeral of Garfield Andrews, the first part of the service being conducted in the Chapel. The full choir was in attendance.

The first part of the funeral service for James Bassett was held at the parish church. The coffin was met at the west door by the vicar, the Reverend S F Marsh, and surpliced choir, who sang in solemn procession the opening sentences of the burial office to a setting by Helmore. The lesson was read by Mr W E Shier (lay reader), and the remainder of the service was taken by the vicar. Among the floral tributes was a wreath from Dorset, sent by Mr and Mrs Reginald Corbett of the Old Malt House, Langton Matravers: 'In deepest admiration for their calling and heartfelt sorrow and sympathy for their dear ones.'

Poor James Bassett's mother, Eliza Annie, whose son was her sole support, received a less welcome message from the Hain Steamship Company:

Expenses incurred on behalf of James Bassett, sailor, drowned 10/1/20, for which the owners are not liable.

R Bartlett bringing corpse from beach and preparing grave for burial at Worth Matravers.	15. 6.
J Smith, coffin & fittings and bringing corpse from Worth to Swanage.	£8.15. 0.
L & SW Railway carriage corpse Swanage to St. Ives Cornwall.	£17.17. 0.
	£27. 7. 6.
Balance wages due	£10.18. 1.

Little wonder then that the following letter should have been written to the editor of the *Western Echo*:

Dear Sir, - Will you grant us a brief space in your local paper to make an appeal to all ex-Service Bluejackets on behalf of our late shipmate T. Noall, who served with us on board H.M.S.

"Albion" during the Dardanelles campaign?

Our late shipmate lost his life in the s.s. Treveal, and we appeal to all our brethren to contribute what little they can to help the widow and three children who are left. Now is everyone's time to act the part of the Good Samaritan, and give to this deserving case as God has given to them.

The names of the collectors of the said brief, which will be known as the "Albion's Fund," are as follows:-

S. Quick, 23, Wesley-place.

W. Trevorrow, Stennack.

W.J. Murt, Fish-street.

N. Tregurtha, Albion House, Back-road-east.

The above will see that proceeds are properly dealt with.

If either collector fails to call personally on anyone who would like to give his mite, it could be left at any of the above addresses. Believing us to be, - Yours truly, boys of the Albion.

St. Ives, Jan. 21st, 1920.

"S.O.S."

The Reverend Horace Piercy, meanwhile, was also receiving letters from relatives of the crew, two fragments of which appeared in Nina Warner Hooke's article (p 13).

The first letter was from Captain Paynter's brother-in-law, James B Walker:

Even now we have not given up hope. I am enclosing a photograph and should esteem it a great favour if you will kindly identify him should it be possible from the enclosed. We would so much like to have his remains and to know where he is resting.

The second was from Peter Cogar's widow, Mary:

Oh, how could they have been so heartless as to leave them so long without assistance? It seems too cruel. He was a devoted husband and father. It was his first and last voyage. We could but ill spare him, he was all we had. Forgive me for writing, and hoping for a reply. Would you tell me if you thought he was tossed about very much in the cruel waves? Please tell me.

Yours truly, a broken hearted mother,

Mary Cogar.

The first page of Horace Piercy's letter in reply to Mrs Cogar is still extant:

Worth
Langton Matravers
Dorset.

Jan. 27th 1920.

Dear Mrs Cogar

Thank you for your kind letter. I wish I could help you in your great sorrow. I do most deeply sympathise with you, & only wish I had been able to give a helping hand to your dear one on that terrible morning. Such men as he must have been can ill be spared. As far as I know nothing was found in his pockets. It would be best for you to write to the vessel's owners, the Hain Steamship Co. Ltd, St. Ives, Cornwall, and ask them to let you have any effects of his which may be recovered from the wreck. Salvage operations are to be begun shortly from Portland. It would be better for you to write, than for me to do so. This will very possibly recover some of his tools in the ship.

From what I saw on the Saturday morning, I should say that the poor man did not have a long fight for life. The seas were terrible, & none of the men were able to live long in it. I feel sure that it was not long after the boat capsized that his soul left his poor body, and was at peace.

If anything is washed up bearing his name or initials, I will send it to you at once.

Chapter 9

'With time on my hands,' wrote Eric Benfield in his book *Southern English* (p 110), 'I was able to develop my inclinations for the delights of beachcombing. Perhaps there is a certain amount of vagabondage in most of us, but beachcombing in Purbeck is entirely divorced from any idea of laziness.'

At Chapman's Pool there used to be two regular beachcombers: both lived alone, and 'combed' alone. Their main haul was planks, washed ashore whenever there had been a heavy 'blow' at sea. Also there was rubbish to be kicked through: battered wicker lobster pots, tins and bottles, shoes, ropes, broom-handles and so on. After the First World War there were a few other prizes that came in with the tide. One beachcomber was once seen bashing the brass horns of a mine with a heavy rock. From time to time a whole cargo found its way into Chapman's Pool. Once a cargo of flour was washed ashore in bags. These had set rock hard, but inside the flour was baking good. Years later a cargo of grapefruit bobbed biliously in the bay; every one as fresh as a first class passenger would expect for breakfast.

A wrecked ship and its crew were a different matter, presenting, to those who were prepared to extend the principle of beachcombing a stage further, the opportunity of a valuable harvest: 'After the troop transporter *William Pitt* had been driven ashore at Chapman's Pool in the Isle of Purbeck in November 1795, the Poole Customs Collector called out the dragoons to escort part of the salvaged cargo and stores "for fear of the violence of the Country people, who had been frustrated in their evil and regular trade"' (Graham Smith: *Hampshire & Dorset Shipwrecks*, p 38). Yet coastal people would attempt to save life - sometimes at great risk to themselves - as much as pillage from the sea; and were often handsomely rewarded for their efforts. When the *Halsewell* was wrecked in 1786: '[the] directors of the company acted quickly, awarding the quarrymen one hundred guineas, a small fortune at the time. The award was to be divided equally among the men who assisted in the rescue' (Steve Shovlar: *Dorset Shipwrecks*, p 23).

In the case of the *Treveal*, after the rescue of the seven survivors, and the hauling in of the bodies in the first 48 hours, nothing human was further recovered by Worth Matravers people. The Hain company made noises to the effect that it hoped that other bodies - and the body of Captain Paynter in particular - might be found; but offered just two shillings and sixpence to anyone who recovered the mortal remains of a sailor of the *Treveal*. Farm workers in 1920 earned about twelve-and-six a week. Thus, the body of Captain Paynter was valued by the Hain company at just a day's wages of a Dorsetshire agricultural labourer.

On two occasions over the years (the two sources being independent of each other) I have heard it said that there was some plundering of sailors' pockets and fingers after the *Treveal* disaster. It may be true but, if so, I have no doubt there was no widespread participation; there were only perhaps two or three villagers of a sufficiently pragmatic bent to take beachcombing to that extreme.

However, the ship was a different matter. Just home from the sub-continent, there was talk of damask tablecloths, Indian silks and carved ivory exotica. While Hains' marine superintendent was 'unable to board the *Treveal* until nine days after she stranded owing to bad weather', it is a matter of record that Chapman's Pool fishing boats visited the wreck much earlier: 'on the morning of the inquest Monty Hooper had rowed out with his daughter Floss to have a look at the wreck ... Floss stayed in the boat while Monty went aboard ... He found the chart room under the bridge quite undamaged ... The stove in the galley was still warm and the bread dry in the oven' (Warner Hooke, p 11). It was the morning of the inquest. Everybody with any authority was gathering at the Square and Compass Inn. All was quiet at Chapman's Pool. Mont Hooper's motive? - according to Cicely Wrixen, 'He was worried if any pet animals were on board' (in Rodney Legg: *Guide to Purbeck Coast and Shipwreck*, p 44).

Bridge of the wrecked Treveal

Mont Hooper's boat may have been the first to visit the wreck, but it was not the last - there was quite a toing and froing, before Hains' marine superintendent ever boarded the vessel. It can be fairly said that while many of the relics from the *Treveal* which found their way into private hands were claimed from the shore to which they were washed by the tide, some were never touched by salt water, far less dashed against rocks.

The two halves of the *Treveal* sat up on the Kimmeridge Ledge throughout the spring and summer of 1920. Most of her cargo of jute was washed ashore, piled higher than a tall man against the cliffs; higher still towards Freshwater Steps. The jute was foul-smelling and covered by tiny flies, which at anyone's approach would swarm into the air as millions of black dots. The stench was all-pervasive, 'higher' even than the fishermen's bait. Many sightseers came to look over the cliff. Some ventured on to the beach. Miss Peggy Patterson was a holiday-maker in 1920: 'I remember one day going down to Chapman's Pool with my brother, sometime after the dreadful Treveal disaster, and feeling terrified of setting foot on the beach. My brother told me I'd tread on arms and legs. There was a lot of jute from the wreck ...' (in E M Wallace: *That's The Way It Was*, p 40). Those who could brave the stench had their rewards. My father found, under some stinking wrack, a gleaming object: a copper buoyancy tank from one of the *Treveal*'s lifeboats. He carried it home to Worth Matravers, where he sold it for five shillings.

The jute lingered at Chapman's Pool for three years, until one winter's night a storm, almost of the ferocity of the hurricane of 1920, swept the beach entirely clean. There was, in the morning, not a whiff of jute; not enough to be collected on a pitchfork the entire length of the beach. Another Chapman's Pool 'stroke'. Stories abound about the Pool. Often, one imagines, because of smuggling, tales were put about, but many have felt that there is an aura about the place and have felt the light tap of an unseen hand on the shoulder. On a fine, hot day, some 50 years after the loss of the *Treveal*, my mother was walking her dog near Chapman's Pool when she met a woman in a state of great agitation. The woman was an artist and had begun to paint the bay when, suddenly, she'd been frozen by a blast of very cold air and overwhelmed by a sense of horror. She had packed up her paints and brushes and was rushing away. My mother began to tell her about the *Treveal*, but the woman continued up the track, calling back that she would never come to the place again.

Cabin door from the Treveal

The Inquiry
Fifth Day - Tuesday, 11 May 1920 - Afternoon

ERNEST GREGORY (Commander of Portland Dockyard), examined by Mr Pilcher, said that on the night of 9 January, knowing that Messrs Collins had no tug available, the Dockyard tug, *Pilot*, was ordered to go out. She was of 615 tons, 1,400 hp and capable of 12 knots in fine weather. Witness stated that he received no SOS message from the *Treveal* after the *Pilot* left Portland shortly after midnight.

By the Court: When he dispatched the *Pilot* he had no thought of saving life. He read the *Treveal*'s message as asking for a tug for general assistance. He thought that if the *Treveal* had wanted a lifeboat she would have asked for it. From the *Treveal*'s later request for lighters and salvage pumps it did not appear that lives were in danger.

Mr Pilcher interposed here that the Board of Trade had requested the Admiralty to arrange for the attendance of Captain Segrave, the Senior Naval Officer at Portland at the time in question.

Mr Wilkinson expressed the opinion that Commander Gregory was in charge and that Captain Segrave could tell no more.

The Court ruled that Captain Segrave should be called.

FREDERICK BURT (Senior Dockyard Pilot at Portland) gave evidence of the sending out of the Dockyard tug *Pilot*. Witness stated that when the tug *Pilot* returned to Portland at midday on 10 January, after her second trip, he notified St Alban's Head that she had left the scene of the wreck on account of the weather and her failure to establish communication with the *Treveal* by signalling. Witness stated that there was a signalman aboard the *Pilot* at all times. The statement of the coastguard that the *Pilot* had no signalman aboard was untrue. Witness described the tug as a 'dirty sea boat'.

(The Court adjourned.)

Sixth Day - Wednesday, 12 May 1920 - Morning

ERNEST BURT (Master of HM Dockyard tug *Pilot*), examined by Mr Pilcher, said that on the night of 9 January his vessel was under two hours' notice for steam. The crew were not all aboard, but the fires were banked and steam could be raised in 20 minutes. Witness received notice of a ship ashore at St Alban's Head and was instructed to proceed there at 10.20 p.m. He called the crew together. Within 40 minutes of the warning he and the crew were aboard, except one man who lived in Weymouth. The *Pilot* left Portland at 12.04 a.m. There was a wind veering from WSW to SW, blowing rather a bad gale, between 30 and 40 mph. It was misty and raining. After leaving the East Entrance of Portland Harbour he set course ESE and went at 12 knots, the full speed of the tug, to look for the *Treveal*. It was then too hazy to see the Shambles light. After a half hour's steaming he was obliged to go to dead slow to allow the men to get the hawser ready. At 12 knots the sea was breaking over the tug. At 1.15 a.m. he resumed full speed, but had to ease up owing to the weather. At 2.30 a.m. he estimated his position to be $2^1/2$ miles south of St Alban's Head. He then eased to dead slow and altered course to the north. He thought he got within a mile or a mile and a half of the Head. He attempted to signal the Head but could get no reply. The signalman tried for 10 or 15 minutes from the bridge with a flash lamp lit by electricity. It had a range of three to five miles in clear weather. He blew his whistle at intervals all the time he was there. It was thick weather and he could not see the light at Anvil Point. Soundings were impossible, the sea was very rough and the tug was making bad weather. He had two feet of water in the hold. He saw no lights at all but imagined he must have passed within two miles of the *Treveal*. Altogether he was nearly an hour lying off St Alban's Head. He thought it would have been dangerous to go nearer the shore than he did in such heavy weather. He shaped course WSW and returned to Portland. He did not see the Shambles light on his return journey and got within half a mile of the Breakwater before he saw the Breakwater light. After making his report, he was ordered to go out again. His original orders were to report his movements to the Dockyard authorities, and being unable to get signals he had had to come right into the harbour. On his second time out he set the same course as previously and saw the *Treveal*'s stern and masthead lights at 7 a.m., just at daybreak, about a mile to the east. The *Treveal* signalled, 'Are you tug?' Witness signalled, 'Yes, What water have you under your stern?' but got no reply. The *Treveal* signalled: 'Heave to and stand by till weather moderates.' The *Treveal* made another signal but visibility was so bad they could not read any part of it. The tug rolled so that it became impossible to keep the glass on her. Witness said he thought he got to within a quarter of a mile of the *Treveal*. He would have risked his tug and crew if he had tried to get any closer, for there were big seas running. His tug drew 12 $1/2$ feet of water. His hawsers were moving about on the deck and there was two feet of water in the forecastle. He was forced to turn her round head to the sea and at 8 a.m. had been blown close under St Alban's Head. The wind was then force 8 or 9. Witness said he saw no flag signals on the *Treveal*. He neither saw nor heard distress rockets. Visibility was very bad. At 9 a.m. a squall struck the *Pilot* and drove her away, and it was not until 10 a.m. that witness caught sight of the *Treveal* again. She was being swept by heavy seas and as witness could do absolutely nothing, he returned to Portland to report. He arrived at Portland at about midday and was sent back out to St Alban's Head at 1 p.m. with six fresh men. He remained off the Head until 10 p.m. He saw the tug *Petrel* on his third trip. She was a smaller boat than witness's and made very bad weather.

Examined by Mr Cunliffe: The only information he had as to the whereabouts of the *Treveal* on the night of 9 January was that she was at St Alban's Head. Telephone inquiry was made of the coastguards at St Alban's and they replied that they knew nothing about a ship ashore but they could see a ship steaming slowly to the eastward, with all lights burning. Witness stated that if he had seen the *Treveal* the first time he went out, he would have stood by, but unless the weather moderated he would have been powerless to help.

By the Court: He was told that an SOS message had been received from the *Treveal*.

Mr Warner: Why did you not call out the lifeboat? - Were you afraid of butting into someone's authority?

Witness: Yes.

Mr Warner: We have heard about people not doing so for fear of being accused of butting in. It's a pity that someone did not warn the lifeboat on this occasion. If the lifeboat had been called, it might have 'butted in' on the wreck and that would have been of great assistance.

By an Assessor: He thought the lifeboat should have been sent out, but did not suggest it to the Senior Dockyard Pilot. The *Pilot* had no rockets, only Verey lights. If he had shown Verey lights, other ships, or coastguards, might have thought he was in distress.

LEWIS WHITE (Mate of the tug *Pilot*), corroborated the evidence of the previous witness.

Examined by Mr Cunliffe: He believed that on the *Pilot*'s second trip the skipper knew that the *Treveal* was on the Kimmeridge Ledge. On the first trip, when they could see nothing, both witness and skipper concluded that the *Treveal* had got off and gone away. Witness stated that it would have been quite impossible to have rendered any assistance to the *Treveal* in the prevailing weather.

WILLIAM ROBERTS (Signalman of the tug *Pilot*) gave evidence of his efforts to call up St Alban's Head on the *Pilot*'s first trip, and of the messages which passed between the *Pilot* and the *Treveal* on the second trip. The only signals he read from the *Treveal* were: 'Are you tug?' and 'Heave to, stand by till weather moderates.' She never told what water she had under her stern, but sent some signals which bad light prevented witness from reading. He continued his efforts to signal her until 10.30 a.m. In his eight years' experience around the coast, he had never known worse weather.

(At the conclusion of the evidence this morning Mr WILKINSON informed the Court that the Senior Naval Officer at Portland on the night of the wreck, Captain Segrave, was now in Rome, and that Captain Segrave's second-in-command on 9/10 January was Commander Rowe who was recently killed in a motor cycle accident near where the Court was presently sitting (Sidney Hall). The COURT decided not to press for Captain Segrave's appearance.)

(The Court adjourned for lunch.)

Afternoon

WILLIAM DONALD (Third Officer of the *Treveal*), recalled, stated that he checked the course half a dozen times before the *Treveal* struck the Kimmeridge Ledge, finding no fault.

By the Court: The *Treveal*'s navigation lights were left on purposely in order to assist in attracting the attention of the tug they thought was coming to their aid. It might possibly have been misleading to anyone approaching or watching. If they had anchored the boats in the lee of the *Treveal* it would have been little good, as the ship broke in two soon after they left.

JOHN DAINTREE (Senior Inspector of Life-Saving Apparatus to the Board of Trade), recalled, said that if the rocket line had been fired over the upturned boats against the strong wind, the line would have bellied upwards and would then have fallen gradually, so that there would have been no question of its tearing along and injuring the men on the boats. Although the rocket apparatus might have been taken down to Chapman's Pool at the outset, witness thought that it was the wiser course to let it remain where it was, until it was known if it would be of use. He had known a vessel followed 15 miles along cliffs.

By Mr Cunliffe: The volunteer company were to a certain extent ignorant of the capabilities of the rocket. They only had quarterly drills.

By the Court: The rocket could have been used at Chapman's Pool with advantage in an effort to save lives.

What happened to the two halves of the *Treveal*? The job of salvaging the cargo, and the vessel's plates and machinery for scrap, was undertaken by Turner Bros of Weymouth, though there was a certain amount of jute saved by Worth Matravers people, done up in bundles for the agent to collect. Turners' tug, *Glenmore*, worked the wreck for the best part of two years. On 24 March 1922 she left Weymouth Harbour for another day's work at the site. A light south-westerly wind was blowing and it had increased somewhat by the time she arrived near the Kimmeridge Ledge. Captain Pavey, the master of the *Glenmore*, decided that work would go ahead. However, the wind grew stronger still and by early afternoon the anchors were beginning to drag. Suddenly, a large swell lifted the *Glenmore* and dumped her on the sharp wreckage of the submerged *Treveal*, splitting open her hull. Captain Pavey ordered the crew to man the pumps and signalled to the St Alban's Head coastguards for assistance. A steam tug, the *Freewill*, and a salvage vessel, the *Albert Victor*, left Weymouth Harbour to go to the aid of the *Glenmore*, but both were forced to return to port, conditions being so bad that they could not get near the stricken vessel. Meanwhile, Captain Pavey realised that the *Glenmore* was doomed. His men were unable to pump out the incoming water fast enough, and he gave the order to abandon ship. No sooner had they pulled away in the lifeboat than the *Glenmore* began to go down. Within a few minutes she had disappeared beneath the waves, together with a considerable quantity of salvage gear, including valuable pumps and lifting apparatus. The crew landed safely at Chapman's Pool, being greeted by Mont Hooper, the Worth Matravers fisherman. Captain Pavey sent word of their safe arrival on shore to the St Alban's Head coastguards and asked them to contact Turner Bros so that transport could be arranged to pick them up. The *Glenmore*'s crew arrived back in Weymouth at eight o'clock that evening.

For some of the survivors of the *Treveal* disaster, salvaging their careers at sea also came to naught. Frank Argall, nephew of the *Treveal* apprentice Frederick Argall wrote to me that, 'The shock of the ship-wreck produced colour-blindness and Fred left the sea.' Fred's brother Charles had taken up the story when I interviewed him on the telephone: 'Fred would have stuck to the sea if he could. He tried a bit of school-mastering but that didn't suit him ... He went to Camborne School of Mining and became a mining engineer, first in South America and later in South Africa, and the story is a sad one because he died at 26.'

Some of those who lost loved ones in the *Treveal* disaster became, in a way, victims themselves. Mrs Eliza Bassett, who received the statement from the Hain company 'Expenses incurred on behalf of James Bassett, sailor, drowned 10/1/20 for which the owners are not liable,' was one such victim. Mrs Quick wrote to me from St Ives: 'Her son's death had a dramatic effect on Eliza Annie, who became an alcoholic and suffered from elephantiasis. This meant spending most of her time in bed as her legs were enormously swollen. I'm sorry to say that the family was not very sympathetic at this stage and my aunt, her niece, was forbidden by her father to visit.'

Lily Stevens of St Ives wrote to me about the family of another drowned sailor, Tom Noall: 'he left a wife Ellen & three young children, Annie 9, Thomas Edward 6 & John Peters 3. His wife Ellen died soon after him aged 38 leaving the three children orphans. Ellen's sister Janie Peters gave up her work in London & came back to St. Ives to bring up the children which she did, in fact she devoted her life to them, it must have been very difficult ...'

Philip Thomas of Saltash wrote to me about Mary Cogar, widow of the *Treveal*'s carpenter, Peter: 'life was hard for Minnie following the death of Peter ... she had four daughters, the eldest of whom, May, would have been about 15 years old at the time of their father's drowning.' The girls' characters were fashioned by the hard times that followed their father's death and the remoteness of Porthoustock. They grew up to be 'Fiercely independent and determined, self-sufficient, thrifty, well able to wield a hammer or saw or drag driftwood up from the beach for the fire ...'

Driftwood ... At Chapman's Pool, a Worth Matravers villager came across a piece of driftwood: a table, finely carved with elephants, which had come from the *Treveal*. Its present owner, having made inquiries as to its origin, was given the opinion that it was not the work of an Indian craftsman, but was made in *imitation* of Eastern style ... by Peter Cogar, the ship's carpenter?

Table top from the Treveal

At Worth Matravers, as in Cornwall, the *Treveal* continued to exert a malevolent influence long after she sank to the bottom of the sea. Was the *Treveal* disaster the final disillusionment which led the Reverend Horace Piercy to leave the Church? He went to teach at a private school in Swanage and, quite soon, 'ran away' with the headmaster's wife.

My grandfather, Frank Lander, as has already been said, could never forget the horror of Chapman's Pool on the terrible morning of 10 January 1920. He died when I was in my teens. I remember my father and mother did watches and when the end was near my mother's whisperings to my father about two pennies and a bandage, something that brought me up short about death: the banality of two pennies and a bandage. So passed a kind, generous spirit and a hard-working, steady man. The one extraordinary event in his life was the *Treveal*. Three things stuck in his mind. First, making off alone to Chapman's Pool and meeting Horace Piercy who was walking back to the village from Weston Farm. Second, and most awful, was that the sailors were so close to the beach: half-naked, crying for help, struggling towards the shore with the already-drowned floating about them - then slipping and sliding on the growling pebbles and whirled out of reach again. The third was an incident on the climb to Mr Gilderdale's cottage. On the shore of the 'Lake' tall bulrushes grew, some as tall as eight feet, and into these Frank had seen a man crawl. In a scene which echoed that between Third Officer Donald and Captain Paynter on the bridge of the *Treveal* the night before, Frank told Horace he had seen someone crawl into the bushes. Horace said he was mistaken; he (Horace) hadn't seen anyone near the reeds. Frank persisted and found one of the crew (Curnow, I think it must have been) rolled up in a ball, shouting to be left there to die.

Frank was really a stone man, a quarryman; it was his wife's family - Grants - who were fishermen. Thus, Frank, married to a fisherman's daughter, took up the trade. Jane had a rather strange attitude towards the *Treveal* and her crew. She seldom spoke about the ship; never, as far as is known, saw it; did not attend the Memorial Service; and later, when relatives of the crew visited from Cornwall, it was Frank who made them welcome, in the little sitting room. The Argalls wanted to give Jane a present, but she wouldn't accept it. The only opinion on the tragedy that she ever expressed was that the crew should have stayed with the ship - that it was wrong to leave her: 'They should have known better than to trust the sea. The sea's easier to get into than out of.' Maybe there was a reason for her wishing to disassociate herself from the event:

superstition. Perhaps she thought that so many drowned sailors would bring bad luck to the fishing grounds. She was alone in her attitude. The village as a whole mourned the dead men. On the Sunday following the loss of the ship, a memorial service was held in Worth Matravers church. Rarely had the church been so full as on that day.

The Inquiry
Seventh Day - Thursday, 13 May 1920 - Morning

Mr PILCHER submitted 16 questions to the Court on behalf of the Board of Trade.

Mr CUNLIFFE addressed the Court with regard to the points affecting the Shipowners. He said the men who sailed in the Hain steamers were drawn very largely from the West of England, more especially St Ives, and the feeling between the company and their employees savoured more of friendship than anything else. The owners had the utmost confidence in the captain and officers of the *Treveal*. He thought the Court would be satisfied from the evidence that the captain and officers were experienced, trustworthy and certificated men; and that the *Treveal* was properly equipped in every way. As to whether proper means were taken, by those concerned, for saving the lives of the men lost in this unfortunate catastrophe, he asked the Court to seriously consider that question. He emphasised certain points for the consideration of the Court. The *Treveal* was observed by the Kimmeridge coastguards, steering an erratic course. Should the *Treveal* not have been warned in some way? With regard to the St Alban's Head coastguards, he submitted that once the *Treveal* was aground it was their duty, as laid down in the coastguard regulations - they had no discretion in the matter - to call out the windward lifeboat. The lifeboat was not called out by the chief officer at St Alban's Head until some 10 hours after the *Treveal* went aground. The volunteer life-saving company in the vicinity was not called out at all. Captain Daintree had stated that the volunteer company ought to have been called out. Then there was the question of the responsibility of the Portland authorities. Within three hours of striking, the *Treveal* sent out two SOS messages, which were received by the warships at Portland. Briefly, what was the duty which devolved upon a person or station or ship when an SOS message was received? It was an urgent signal and one which should not be disregarded. He suggested that it was the duty of the authority receiving an SOS signal to take all precautions to render assistance to the vessel which sent out the SOS. The question was - was that done in this case?

No evidence had been afforded as to what officer (if any) in a responsible position received the SOS and what was done by that officer when the message was received. The acting harbourmaster, Commander Gregory, took a certain course, but said he would not take any steps to save life by sending for the lifeboat because it was not his business to do so; he would be afraid of 'butting in' to some other authority. What he did was to send out the tug *Pilot*. The master of the tug had told the Court that he could not render any assistance. He (Mr Cunliffe) ventured to suggest that the evidence showed that if the lifeboat had been called out earlier it could have gone round under the leeside of the *Treveal* and saved everyone on board. It was not a question of attacking individuals in any way, but if by a recommendation of that Court the authorities might be made more alive to the utility of those men in similar circumstances the recommendation of the Court would have done great service to the shipping world and to those 'who go down to the sea in ships.' He suggested, too, that there should be more protecting lights between Portland Breakwater and Anvil Point - or some bell on the cliff which might be used to warn ships away from the shore.

Mr WILKINSON, replying on behalf of the Admiralty, first dealt with the criticism of the coastguard service, and said it was not realised by the men at St Alban's Head that the *Treveal* was in any imminent danger; she was burning all her lights, she had only asked for tugs and it was not until 8 or 9 o'clock in the morning that her flag signals were seen. As to the regulation about the calling out of the windward lifeboat the station officer had told them his construction of the words in that regulation. It might be that the authorities would now make the regulation more explicit than it was. If it was a wrong construction then it was an error of judgment. So far as the St Alban's Head coastguards were concerned, all that they knew that the *Treveal* asked for was tugs. He agreed that it was unfortunate that the volunteer company was not called out, but he submitted that it would not have been a wise thing to send the rocket apparatus down to Chapman's Pool. He then dealt with the question of the tug, and submitted that the master did all he possibly could under the circumstances. All that the Portland authorities were asked to do was to send a tug. They could not have everybody notifying a lifeboat. The naval authorities knew that the coastguards were in communication with the vessel and they were entitled to assume that the coastguards had taken the necessary action as laid down in their regulations.

Mr PILCHER said that any recommendations which the Court might make would be received with respect by the proper authorities and dealt with, but any change in any system of great importance would have to be considered by the departmental authorities after consultation with experts. He then shortly summed up the evidence. With regard to the naval authorities and the calling out of the lifeboat, whether they were going by some regulation he did not know; but it might well be that as members of the public as well as members of the naval service, they might have exercised more imagination and warned the lifeboat. Mr H J GROVES (President): I should like, now that the inquiry is closed, to thank all those concerned who have come forward to help the Court through all these long days of sitting, and to express, what everyone feels, our great grief at what happened on that fateful day, 9 January. The secret of how that ship came on the Ledge is lost in Chapman's Pool. There is no doubt about that. All I can say is that it is extraordinary. The Court would like me to say, with regard to the survivors, that no responsibility rests on them. It was an awful day and an awful fatality, and it is shrouded in mystery. It seems inexplicable and marvellous in these days of modern appliances. Here is a mechanically-propelled ship, and about here we have the telephone, telegraph, wireless, coastguards and lifeboats, all in the vicinity of a great naval and mercantile port; and yet this could have happened in not abnormal weather and the lives of 36 men out of 43 be lost - men who all through the war, no doubt, like the brave mercantile marine, of which we are all so proud, did their duty as heroes, running the gauntlet of a ruthless and unscrupulous enemy - coming home from Calcutta to Dundee, just calling at Portland for a North Sea pilot, which they were unable to get, expecting shortly to meet their dear ones again, and in a few hours' time they lost their lives in this way. It is not judicial what I am saying, but I cannot help expressing it. We have one redeeming feature, perhaps, and that is the bravery of those British men who saved the lives of four of them. I refer to the clergyman and to Frank Lander. I ask the Court to rise and express our sincere condolence with the relatives and friends of those who lost their lives.

(It was announced that the Court would deliver its Judgment on Monday, 17 May.)

Monday, 17 May 1920

(An official notice was posted at Weymouth Guild Hall that judgment would not be made known for a few days. No reason was given for the delay.)

The Memorial Service for the drowned sailors of the *Treveal*, held on the Sunday after the disaster, at Worth Matravers parish church, was a church and chapel congregation and the pews were full.

The Reverend Piercy conducted the service and it seemed he chose the opening hymn carefully:

> God moves in a mysterious way
> His wonders to perform;
> He plants his footsteps in the sea,
> And rides upon the storm.

The hymn was written by W Cowper, who wrote 'The Castaway', a poem which depicts, with tragic power, the suffering of a seaman, swept overboard and awaiting death by drowning.

Maybe in the solemn gloom of the church, some of the congregation looked around for their critics, those who it seemed had expected the very Ledge itself to call up to the village for help.

The curate then asked for a minute's silence. In the prayers that followed the congregation was asked to remember Almighty God who, for the sins of man, once drowned all the world except for eight persons.

Hardly had the church door closed on the service than a kind of amnesia set in. Neither Frank Lander nor his daughter Daisy would ever be able to recall a word of the Reverend Piercy's sermon; though the pew at which they sat would be remembered clearly by both for the rest of their days.

Chapter 10

The Inquiry

Report of Court - Wednesday, 19 May 1920

Mr H J GROVES (President): The Court finds that the loss of the *Treveal* was caused by her stranding on Kimmeridge Ledge on the night of 9 January 1920, due to some error in navigation, which, owing to the lamentable death of the master, the Court is unable to definitely ascertain. The loss of life was immediately due to the two boats containing the officers and crew of the *Treveal* being overturned in the surf in Chapman's Pool while they were attempting to reach the shore.

The Court is of opinion that the heavy loss of life would not have occurred had the Weymouth, or windward lifeboat, been called out, and the volunteer life-saving company at Worth Matravers summoned when the stranding of the *Treveal* was first known on shore.

[The President proceeded to give the Court's answers to the 16 questions posed by counsel for the Board of Trade:]

1. What was the cost of the vessel to her owners? What was her value at the time she was lost? What insurances were effected upon the ship?

The cost of the vessel to her owners in September 1919, when she was built, was £170,000. Her value at the time she was lost was £250,000. No insurances were effected upon the ship.

2. What compasses had the vessel? When and by whom were they last adjusted? Were they sufficient for the safe navigation of the vessel, and were the errors on the various courses ascertained by observation from time to time?

The vessel had two Kelvin Compasses in position, the Standard in the top of the wheel house, and the Steering Compass in the wheel house. They were last adjusted by Kelvin, Bottomley & Baird in the Clyde on 9 September 1919. They were sufficient for the safe navigation of the vessel, and the errors in the various courses were ascertained by observation from time to time.

3. When the vessel last left Calcutta was she supplied with: (a) proper and sufficient boats and life-saving appliances? (b) proper and sufficient means for making signals of distress if she required assistance?

(a) When the vessel last left Calcutta she was supplied with proper and sufficient boats and life-saving appliances. (b) She also had proper and sufficient means for making signals of distress if she required assistance.

4. When did the vessel arrive off Portland? What was the position at the time of leaving? What courses were steered thereafter? At the time of and after leaving Portland was the master of the *Treveal* on the bridge in charge of the navigation of the vessel?

The vessel arrived off Portland at about 6 p.m. on 9 January 1920. According to the evidence of the master of the *St Keverne*, which the Court thinks reliable, the vessel was lying about 1 1/2 miles to the northeast of Eastern Entrance to Portland Harbour when he took the letters on board and the vessel then sailed. There is no evidence to show what course was steered from this point of departure until the Shambles light was abeam. When the light was abeam at 8.07 p.m. on 9 January the course being steered was SE by E 1/2 E by compass, which was intended to make SE by E magnetic, and this course was continued until shortly before she struck, when it was altered half a point to the southward. The master was on the bridge in charge of the navigation of the vessel.

5. Where did the vessel strand at or about 9 p.m. on 9 January last? How far was she from the shore?

The vessel stranded at or about 9 p.m. on 9 January last on the southeast edge of the Kimmeridge Ledge in a position with Chapman's Pool bearing about E by N (magnetic) and St Alban's Head Flag Staff S 52 E (magnetic) 1 1/10 mile. She was distant from the nearest shore 1/2 mile, but to the place where some of the crew landed 8/10 of a mile.

6. After stranding: What lights did the vessel show? What wireless or other messages if any were sent out and received by her, and when? By what stations were they picked up, and to what stations or bases were they transmitted?

All the navigation lights were kept burning until the dynamo stopped at about 8 o'clock the next morning. At about 10 p.m., to facilitate getting the boats ready, cluster lights were exhibited at the davit heads, the after part of the bridge over the well deck. Five clusters in all were used and after the boats were got ready some cluster lights were turned seawards. These and all possible lights were kept burning until the dynamo stopped next morning shortly after daylight.

Flashing signals sent out and received by the *Treveal* shortly after midnight, 9/10 January 1920:

Coastguard St Alban's Head to *Treveal*: 'What ship is that?'

Treveal to St Alban's Head coastguard: 'SS *Treveal* from Calcutta to Dundee, ashore hard and fast, is there a good landing place?'

Coastguard St Alban's Head to *Treveal*: 'There is a landing place straight inshore from you; it would be better to wait till daylight if possible.'

4.50 a.m.:

Treveal to St Alban's Head coastguard: 'Will you please phone Portland. Tug has not yet arrived.'

(Message phoned to Portland who replied 'Tug has returned having failed to find ship and having no signalman on board, but was leaving again immediately.' Note: 'Having no signalman on board' is entered by St Alban's Head coastguard, but not confirmed by evidence of Senior Dockyard Pilot, nor is it probable, as there was a signalman on board: but may have been confused with the statement: 'Tug not fitted with wireless.')

5 a.m. to 7 a.m.:

Coastguard St Alban's Head called up the *Treveal* at intervals, but could get no acknowledgement, though the *Treveal*'s lights were quite plain.

[The President recited the various wireless messages sent to and received from the *Treveal*, and indicated that the signals between the *Treveal* and the tug *Pilot* would be given in answer to question 9. The President continued:]

7. When was there immediate danger to the ship and/or crew? Did she make signals of distress? If so, what were they and when and to whom were they made?

In view of the fact that it was winter, a dark night, a south-west wind, and the speed at which the ship was going, the Court is of opinion that there was immediate danger to the ship and crew directly she struck. No distress signals, rockets, or flares were shown through the night. At about 8 a.m. flag signals were hoisted, two of which were urgent, and one vocabulary, viz:

AG I must abandon ship.

NR I want assistance remain by me.

PYL Keep as close as you can to pick up my boats.

They were made to the tug *Pilot* and to the shore signal stations. About the same time four distress rocket signals were sent up.

8. What information reached the coastguards or the naval authorities with regard to the vessel being ashore and/or in danger? What action was taken upon such information?

The first information that reached the naval authorities with regard to the vessel being ashore was the WT message 21.51 ('Urgent. G H Collins, Portland. Send tug boat to St Alban's Head. *Treveal* ashore.') The Government tug *Pilot* was ordered out. At 11 p.m. St Alban's Head coastguard station received a message from Portland via Lulworth 'Treveal ashore near St Alban's Head, tug coming to her assistance.' This was the first intimation the coastguards received. This message was passed to the coastguard, Swanage, for the divisional officer, but was not delivered to him until 8.40 a.m. on 10 January. Kimmeridge was also advised. [The President recited again the flashing signals that passed between the St Alban's coastguard and the *Treveal* shortly after midnight and continued:] The coastguards took no further action beyond keeping a look out on the ship.

9. Was there any undue delay in sending the tug *Pilot* from Portland to the assistance of the vessel? How was it she did not locate the vessel on her first trip? At what time on her second trip did the tug locate the vessel? What signals passed between the tug and the ship?

There was no undue delay in sending the tug *Pilot* from Portland to the assistance of the vessel. The tug was under two hours' notice, and left a quarter of an hour before the expiration of that time. The tug did not locate the vessel on the first trip firstly, because of thick weather, which besides reducing visibility caused the tug to be navigated with caution and possibly not to approach the coast near enough, and secondly, when the tug turned northward she was too far to the eastward of the wreck. At about 7 a.m. on her second trip the tug located the *Treveal* when she saw the masthead and stern lights about a mile to the eastward. The following flashing signals passed between the tug and the ship:

From *Treveal*: 'Are you tug?'

From tug: 'Yes, what water have you got under your stern? (No answer.)

From *Treveal*: 'Heave to, stand by till weather moderates.'

The *Treveal* started another signal which the tug could not take in. After this no more signalling took place.

10. In the circumstances was it practicable for the tug to render assistance to the vessel at any time, and when? If so, did she render such assistance, and if she rendered no assistance how was it she did not do so?

In the circumstances it was not practicable for the tug to render any assistance to the vessel itself, but had she located the vessel on the first trip whilst the weather was still moderate, and the master of the *Treveal* concurred, it is possible she might have got hold of her boats and thus saved the crew. The tug rendered no assistance because she had not located the ship when the weather was comparatively moderate, and in the second trip the weather conditions were too bad.

11. Was a proper watch kept on the vessel whilst she was ashore by the coastguards at Kimmeridge and St Alban's Head coastguard stations?

A proper watch was kept on the vessel whilst she was ashore by the coastguards at Kimmeridge and St Alban's Head, though on account of the thickness of the weather this was somewhat futile, but when the *Treveal* was approaching, a signal should have been made by the coastguard at St Alban's Head that she was standing into danger.

12. Were the distress or other signals shown or made by the vessel seen or heard by any of the coastguards? If so, by whom and at what times? If not, how was it that they were not seen or heard?

The distress rockets fired by the *Treveal* were not seen because they were fired in daylight and thick weather. They were not heard by the coastguards on account of the direction of the wind carrying their sound up the valley, Hill Bottom, towards Worth Matravers where they were heard. The flashing signals made during the night were taken in by St Alban's Head. The flag signals made about 8 a.m. were taken in by St Alban's Head.

13. At what time on the morning of 10 January last did the crew of the *Treveal* take to the boats and attempt to land? Was the fact known to the coastguards stationed at Kimmeridge and St Alban's Head? If not, were measures taken by the coastguards to watch for and meet the boats and assist the crew to land? If not, why not?

Shortly after 9 a.m. on 10 January the crew of the *Treveal* took to the boats and attempted to land at Chapman's Pool. The actual fact of the crew leaving the *Treveal* in boats was not known to the coastguard at either station. Their intention to abandon ship was known to the coastguard at St Alban's Head by reading the flag signals at 8.40 a.m. The information reached the Kimmeridge coastguard about 9 a.m. when two men were sent along the coast to render assistance, but this was too late to be of effect. St Alban's coastguard appears to have taken no action beyond keeping a look out on the ship for the boats leaving her. Having acquainted the ship during the night that 'there was a landing place at Chapman's Pool but it was better to wait till daylight if possible,' the coastguard at St Alban's Head should have appreciated the situation and called out the volunteer life-saving company and sent them to Chapman's Pool.

14. Having regard to the position of the ship when ashore, could the rocket apparatus have been used with any chance of success? Were the rocket company called out, and if not, why not? In the circumstances

might their services have been of value in saving life?

Having regard to the position of the *Treveal* when ashore the rocket apparatus could not have been used on her. Until it was appreciated that the vessel was hard and fast where she struck it would have been inadvisable to move the rocket apparatus from St Alban's Head, but after that the rocket apparatus might have been used with some success on the boats and at least have minimised the loss of life. The rocket company was not called out, as stated in answer to question 13. The reason they were not called out was due to a grave error of judgment on the part of the coastguard at St Alban's Head. Under the circumstances their services would have been of great value in saving life, even if the rocket itself was not used.

15. What was the cause of the loss of the vessel and the loss of life, and how did the survivors from the crew succeed in getting ashore? What assistance was rendered to any of them, and by whom?

The cause of the loss of the vessel was the stranding on Kimmeridge Ledge. This was due to some error in navigation, which, owing to the lamentable death of the master we are unable to ascertain. The conditions prevailing at the time rendered salvage of the ship impossible. The loss of life was caused by the boats being overturned in the surf. Three of the survivors succeeded in getting ashore themselves. Four were gallantly rescued by the Reverend Mr Piercy and Mr Frank Lander. Mr Piercy and Mr Lander were the only people who assisted in getting the survivors out of the water.

16. When was the lifeboat at Weymouth or elsewhere warned? Was such warning given in time for assistance to be rendered. Should any warning have been given earlier, and if so by whom? When warned, was the Weymouth lifeboat promptly launched, and did she do all that was possible in the circumstances?

The message warning the Weymouth lifeboat was received by the coxswain at 9.40 a.m. on 10 January, having been passed through Weymouth coastguard from the coastguard at St Alban's Head, after reading the flag signals at 8.40 a.m. This warning was not in time for assistance to be rendered nor was any other lifeboat warned. The warning ought to have ben given by the coastguard at St Alban's Head on the evening of 9 January, directly he knew that the ship was on shore (Coastguard Instructions 1911: paragraph 5, article 673) and might have been given at the same time from Portland Dockyard and Messrs Collins. When warned the lifeboat was promptly launched and did nearly all that was possible in the circumstances, but the Court think that the lifeboat, when it arrived at the wreck, might have gone in closer to the leeward of the vessel, when the coxswain would have ascertained that the boats had left the ship, and might have been led to proceed towards Chapman's Pool with the intention of assisting any men on the boats or in the water. It is observed that the coxswain stated that the lifeboat arrived about 11.30 whilst the last survivor was rescued at the beach at about 11.20 a.m. There may still have been others in the water alive.

[The President reviewed the evidence relating to the ownership and seaworthiness of the *Treveal* and gave a narrative of the events of 9/10 January. The President then proceeded to deliver the Opinion of the Court on the cause of the stranding and loss of the ship and life:]

The actual point of departure from Weymouth Bay is of importance in ascertaining the cause of the stranding.

William Torrance, coxswain of the *St Keverne*, who brought letters to the *Treveal* just before she proceeded, left Portland Harbour by the North Entrance to close the ship, which he states was lying in a position NE $^{1}/_{2}$ E, 1 $^{1}/_{2}$ miles from the Breakwater Lighthouse. Alfred Spranklin, coxswain of the Weymouth lifeboat, who was standing on Weymouth Pier when the vessel left, placed her a mile to the south of the above position; but the position he marked on the chart differs from what he stated verbally. R H W Thirkell, chief engineer of the *Treveal*, placed her still further south; but this was merely the result of casual observation by a non-expert.

Therefore the Court accepts the position, viz - NE $^{1}/_{2}$ E, 1 $^{1}/_{2}$ miles from Portland Breakwater Lighthouse, as being approximately correct for the point of departure.

The master of the *Treveal* in giving the compass course SE by E $^{1}/_{2}$ E to the third officer, stated there was half a point easterly deviation and the magnetic course would be SE by E. From the accepted point of departure SE by E (magnetic) would have been a safe course, though perhaps rather fine. The master of the *Treveal* may have had records of observations for deviation which were lost with the ship. From the 'compass observation' book recovered, five observations in latitude 32 to 37 N, on SE $^{3}/_{4}$ E and SE by E courses, were: 1 E, 1 E, 1 E, 1 W, 3 W.

Had the deviation been half a point *West* instead of half a point *East* (as applied), the magnetic course would have been ESE. This course, if steered from the accepted point of departure would have passed close to the position given by the chief officer at Kimmeridge coastguard station for 8.40 p.m., viz - three miles west of the station, and almost exactly on to the spot where the *Treveal* struck the ground. Taking into consideration the last deviation of which records were produced was 3 W the Court considers it most probable that a deviation of the wrong name was applied and the course ESE (magnetic) made in consequence, which led the ship to danger. The flood tide acting on the starboard side would have set the ship slightly towards land. There is no record of the methods taken by the master to check his positions on leaving Weymouth Bay. The distance two miles off the Shambles light when abeam, is evidently an error; Alfred Spranklin who was watching the ship from Weymouth Pier stated she was much further off.

Had the course been altered boldly to the southward instead of only half a point when the loom of the land was seen the disaster might have been averted.

The absence of any signal from the coastguard station at St Alban's Head warning the ship that she was standing into danger, may have contributed, though, from the times given in the evidence, it is doubtful if the coastguard could have done so in time to avert the catastrophe.

It is much to be regretted that the *Treveal* made no distress signals - such as firing rockets, burning blue lights or flares - during the night. Such might have awakened the coastguard to the need for calling the lifeboat and volunteer life-saving company; and if made about the time the tug was expected, would have disclosed the ship's position to her.

The coastguard at St Alban's Head showed throughout a lamentable lack of appreciation of the situation.

Having been informed by Kimmeridge station that a vessel was standing towards St Alban's Head, steering an erratic course, and seeing both bow lights of the approaching vessel, St Alban's Head should have made the warning signal that the ship was standing into danger.

On first learning that the ship was ashore, as she was on the edge of the Ledge and had made no distress signals, this station may have been justified in thinking the vessel might get off; but, at any rate, should have warned the lifeboats in the vicinity, or at least the windward boat at Weymouth. Unfortunately, the Coastguard Instructions on this point are ambiguously worded; and in the absence of distress signals, the chief officer thought that, though on shore, the ship was not in distress and that therefore he need not call the lifeboat.

From his local knowledge of the dangers of the coast, especially in the increasing bad weather from the southward, the chief officer at St Alban's Head should have known that a vessel in the situation of the

Treveal was in danger, and informed the lifeboat, whether distress signals were made or not.

He should have informed Kimmeridge station of the message received soon after midnight that the *Treveal* had inquired about a landing place in order that Kimmeridge coastguard, which is responsible for the coastline between that station and St Alban's Head, could take steps to watch the coast, and assist the landing.

He should also have called out the volunteer life-saving company in readiness to assist the landing.

The Court did not believe that either Chief Officer Keeley or Charles Newman, captain of the volunteer life-saving company at Worth Matravers, entertained the opinion (erroneous as it was) of the danger of the use of the rocket which they ventured to put before the Court.

The coastguards at Kimmeridge appear to have done as much as they could on the information received, but might have ascertained from St Alban's Head whether the lifeboat had been informed or done it independently.

The coastguards at Swanage should have passed messages received re a ship on shore to the divisional officer immediately. The latter could then have taken part in the direction of affairs and supplied some of the intelligence lacking in his subordinates in time to minimise the loss of life. Though he seems to have displayed a lack of energy until after he had received a message that lives had been lost.

The naval authorities at Portland promptly rendered assistance, dispatching the tug *Pilot*, but should have warned the lifeboat that a ship was ashore, especially after the receipt of the first SOS wireless signal.

A co-ordination of the Admiralty, Board of Trade, and civil organisations is indispensable.

More efficient instructions for the warning of the lifeboat are necessary.

Clear orders that the lifeboat should be warned whenever a ship is on shore should be displayed in a conspicuous position in coastguard stations, so there may be no doubt as to the action taken, which should not be left to individual discretion.

Instructions should be given to the naval authorities at Portland to warn the lifeboat as soon as they have knowledge that a ship is ashore.

The coastguards should be enjoined to make themselves thoroughly acquainted directly they join a station with the dangers in the vicinity, the methods of saving life in the various situations that may arise, and the best methods of locomotion to various points.

Except that he should have burnt a blue light or similar signal to attract attention when he failed to find the *Treveal*, or to communicate with St Alban's Head coastguard, and that he might, by the use of the lead, have approached the land closer, the Government tug *Pilot* did all that was possible under the existing circumstances and weather conditions.

The Court's opinion on the action of the Weymouth lifeboat was fully stated in the answer to question 16.

Whilst the Court recognises that the saving of life in the case of shipwreck is not the primary duty of the coastguard, it regrets that the small complement of the coastguard stations prevents them from rendering efficient aid in the absence for any reason of the volunteer life-saving company.

On the night in question the station at St Alban's Head was short of complement by two men who were on leave. The remainder were inadequate for any other duty but signalling.

The Court considers that the complement of the coastguard stations should be increased, all of whom should be intelligent and capable men.

The inefficiency of the coastguard telephonic communication, especially near Swanage, was made apparent by this inquiry.

The Court recommends that immediate steps be taken to render telephonic communication efficient in any state of weather.

The Court also considers that a telephone between St Alban's Head coastguard station and some central point at Worth Matravers would be of great value in summoning the volunteer company in emergency.

The Court wishes to call particular attention to the brave and gallant conduct of the Reverend H M Piercy and Mr F Lander in rescuing the survivors under circumstances of great difficulty.

Court Martial
Portsmouth - Friday, 13 August 1920

Mr Frederick Keeley, chief petty officer belonging to His Majesty's ship *Victory*, Coastguard Section, was charged, first, with on 9 January last negligently performing the duty imposed upon him when in charge of St Alban's Head coastguard station in not taking the necessary steps to inform the authorities connected with the windward lifeboat that the steamship *Treveal* was ashore on Kimmeridge Ledge, off St Alban's Head, as directed by paragraph 5, article 673, of the Coastguard Instructions, 1911 ('In the event of a Coast Guard Officer or man observing a vessel in distress (including vessels ashore) or signals of distress, or hearing guns denoting a vessel in distress, he will at once take the necessary steps to inform the authorities connected with the windward Life-Boat, either by telephone or telegraph, as the case may be, unless he should consider the circumstances require the launch of another Life-Boat or other Life-Boats in which case he will advise the authorities of such Life-Boat or Life-Boats accordingly.'); and, secondly, that he did on 10 January 1920, negligently perform the duty imposed upon him in not using his utmost endeavours to save the lives of the master and crew of the steamship *Treveal*, wrecked on Kimmeridge Ledge, off St Alban's Head, as directed by paragraph 1, article 633, of the Coastguard Instructions, 1911 ('All Officers and men of the Coast Guard are to render every possible assistance to vessels in distress, and in cases of shipwreck to use their utmost endeavours to save the lives of the persons on board, and to save and protect from plunder and embezzlement the rigging, sails, stores, and cargo.').

Captain Palmer, HMS *Vernon*, was President of the Court, sitting with Paymaster Rear-Admiral F J Krabbe, Deputy Judge Advocate of the Fleet.

The prisoner, who pleaded 'Not guilty', was assisted by Lieutenant-Commander Smith Wright, Coastguard Divisional Officer, stationed at Swanage. Captain Fawcet Wray, DSO, captain of Portsmouth Coastguard area, prosecuted.

The circumstantial letter recalled the role of the prisoner in the events of 9/10 January, and a number of witnesses were called in support of the prosecution.

The prisoner in his defence disclaimed primary responsibility, although when questioned by the coastguard captain six months ago he accepted responsibility. If he had had any idea at the time what consequences such acceptance of responsibility would entail for him he would not have taken it. He contended that responsibility in the affair should really rest upon the station within whose area the accident occurred. In reply to the charges he submitted that the wording of the instructions was vague. A vessel ashore was not necessarily a vessel in distress. So far as his information went the *Treveal* was not in distress when stranded. He had no information that she had been making SOS signals by wireless. The flag signals were clearly addressed to the tug. He thought the latter would have closed the *Treveal*, and if the *Treveal*'s crew left her then the boats would make for the tug. If the master of the *Treveal* had adopted his advice, and left the ship at first light, the boats could have got ashore in safety. He did not call the volunteer company because the *Treveal* lay so far off that the rocket apparatus could not be used. He was in charge of an important war signal station, and as he had only four men under him he considered he would not have been justified in sending any of them to Chapman's Pool unless he was sure that their services were needed there.

The Court found both charges proved, and ordered the prisoner to be dismissed his ship, the *Victory*, and to be severely reprimanded.

Chapter 11

It was all over. A ship had gone aground and 36 lives had been lost. After two coroner's inquests, a Board of Trade inquiry and a court martial, it had been established, as far as was possible, what had gone wrong; and the guilty parties - or, to be precise, Frederick Keeley, station officer at St Alban's Head - had been punished. There was some subsequent debate as to whether or not Keeley was merely a scapegoat, but the question which has lingered longer than any other is: How did the *Treveal* come to go aground in the first place? The court of inquiry found that the stranding was 'due to some error in navigation, which, owing to the lamentable death of the master, the Court is unable to definitely ascertain.' I held out little hope of discovering anything more but determined, nevertheless, to follow up anything I could to do with Captain Paynter and Third Officer Donald.

I sent off to the National Maritime Museum for the captain's certificates of competency and I arranged to visit the third officer's son, Malcolm Donald, at Swansea. I hoped Mr Donald might remember something more, or that his elder sister, who he said he would speak to before my visit, might have some new information. I also planned to revisit St Ives to follow up William Donald's post-*Treveal* career with the Hain line in the company ledgers, and to see if Captain Kemp would give me his opinion on what could have gone wrong on the ship's bridge on the night of 9 January.

It was a dark December evening when I arrived at Swansea. I found myself on a long seafront road of guest houses, and tired after the long drive resolved to get my accommodation sorted out straight away, without worrying whether I was anywhere near the address - Mr Donald's - which I would be visiting the next day. I parked the car and wandered the seafront, weighing up the various guest houses, the big front windows of each warmly inviting, landlords idly polishing glasses behind little bars, and each house having tried to outdo its neighbour for the quantity, diversity and garishness of its Christmas decorations. I gave up trying to discriminate between them and walked back to the one nearest my parked car.

Mr Donald and his wife kindly welcomed me into their home in a quiet cul-de-sac in the Uplands district of Swansea. We sat at a table in the kitchen, looking out of large patio door windows on a well-kept garden. Mr Donald, I thought, looked very much his father's son. He told me again the things he had told me over the telephone and showed me the Bible which his father reputedly had on him when the crew abandoned ship. The interview proceeded:

Q. Have you remembered anything else at all since we spoke on the telephone?

A. No, and I've spoken to both my sisters and they can't remember anything either.

Q. Nothing at all?

A. My father had a half-brother - he might not still be alive now - who lived somewhere in this area at one time and he had a son a similar age to me, but we lost touch. These things happen ... Some things come back to you and lots of other things you tend to forget.

Q. What sort of a lady was your mother?

A. A little dut. Four foot and a bit, she was a tiny lady, and jolly. They were quite a big family my mum's family. Her maiden name was Davis.

Q. Do you know how she and your father met?

A. No. (Laughs.) I wasn't around at the time.

Q. You said your father became a pilot here at Swansea. Do you know if he sailed with any other line after Hains before he became a pilot?

A. I'm afraid I don't know anything at all about that.

Q. In his photograph, your father looks a man of a very cheerful disposition -

A. I can't remember. I know I've got a photograph somewhere messing around with him under the bonnet of a car ...

Q. He had a car, then?

A. He had to have a car to get backwards and forwards to the docks see. There wasn't any transport in the middle of the night. He used to have his own car and of course there was no drink and drive in those days.

Q. I suppose not ... You said on the phone your father died in tragic circumstances ... I wonder would you mind telling me about that?

A. He used to have these call-outs late at night to bring a ship in - because of course it depends on the tide - and on this particular occasion he went, he must have had a slurp with the skipper - a noggin of some description - and when he got back he slept in the lounge on the settee and must have fallen asleep smoking, and that was it, unfortunately - and that was July nineteen-thirty ... seven.

Q. Was it a fire, then, or -

A. Yes, a fire - set the settee alight. We children were lucky to get out of the house, on to a flat roof at the back of the house, and my sister cut her arm smashing the window.

Q. Was there an inquest?

A. I think we've got a report. Now where it is I don't know ...

I reached the Swansea library 10 minutes before closing time, got the *South Wales Evening Post* for 1937 on the microfilm reader and searched through the month of July for a report on William Donald's death. Eventually, I found it, Saturday, 24 July: 'Swansea Fire Drama Heroism - POLICEMAN CRAWLS INTO BLAZING KITCHEN - "COMPLETE MYSTERY" OF FIRE NOT SOLVED AT INQUEST - VERDICT ON HARBOUR PILOT'. The library clock was ticking on. I had a few minutes left and scribbled notes as fast as I could:

William John Donald, of 25, Maple-crescent, Uplands, Swansea ... "Death due to carbon-monoxide poisoning, brought about through inhaling the fumes from burning furniture, and shock following extensive burns." ... no evidence to show how the fire was caused ... Donald was a harbour pilot, and on the morning when the fire broke out his wife was away on holiday in Pembroke ... Mrs Elsie Mabel Donald ... She received a letter from her husband on the Tuesday, Wednesday and Thursday. In one letter he wrote that he was 'whacked for the want of sleep.' Her husband was a heavy sleeper, because he was tired after his duties, and if he only had a few hours off he would often sleep on the settee downstairs so as not to disturb her and the household ... her husband was a heavy smoker, and sometimes would smoke in bed, and also on the settee ... possible that he would drop off to sleep on the settee when smoking ... David M Malyn, a student, who lived near, said he was friendly with Donald and was frequently in his company ... arrangement that he would meet Donald that evening to take him in his car to the docks. He met Donald at 7 o'clock, and they went to the Exchange Restaurant ... left Donald there and called back for him about 8.45. Donald was then perfectly sober ... went to Rutland-street, where he left Donald in the street while he went to an hotel ... did not see Donald again ... Thomas Turner, a barman at the Rutland Hotel, said Donald left that hotel about 9.30. He had had a few glasses of beer but was not under the influence of drink in any way, and was fully capable of taking care of himself. Just before 11 p.m.

there was a knock at the hotel door, and when he opened it he saw
Donald, who said he wished to see the licensee, but he told
Donald the licensee was out and shut the door, leaving Donald
in the street ... ['The library is now closing,' said a voice close by.]
... coroner said ... he must gave gone home ... nothing to show
how the fire originated ...

Poor Donald. The thought kept coming into my head as I drove back to
Dorset. It was a wild night. The rain poured out of the sky and the wind
buffeted the car. I kept my eyes fixed on the white lines in the centre of
the road. Poor Donald, I was thinking, when the road suddenly opened
out either side of me, a vast expanse of tarmac like an airport, and the
car snaked as my preoccupied mind decided which of 6, 7, 8, 9 - I gave
up counting - lanes to proceed in. The approach to the Severn Bridge
was empty on this December night. The huge structure itself was
invisible in the darkness, its enormity suggested all the more
compellingly by the illuminated toll gates, and lines of lights leading
upwards, as if Man in his vanity imagined he could defy Nature and
build for himself a gateway to the Heavens. The bridge swung in the
storm and I wondered whether I should ever have ventured onto it.
Poor Donald, I thought, poor Donald. Twice in his life he had fallen foul
of two of Nature's fundamental elements: a sea that had raged against
and humiliated 3,000 tons of man's finest engineering, as well as the
flesh and bone of that which had been made in God's image; and then
the fire, the element of hell itself, in which he had perished. As a boy at
Worth Matravers I had taken comfort from the sea outside the chapel
door, all ready, I thought, to rush in and quench hell's fire - but now I
wondered which was the worse fate. Poor Donald, I thought ...

I was waiting for copies of Captain Paynter's certificates of competency
from the National Maritime Museum, before I headed off again to St
Ives. The Christmas period prolonged the wait and by the time 10
January came around - which meant two years and three anniversaries
of working on the *Treveal* story - I was still waiting. The day barely
dawned, so dark was it. Storm warnings had ben broadcast and I
decided to walk out into the weather to remind myself what Chapman's
Pool was like on such a day. I thought I would go via St Alban's Head,
but the wind was so ferocious on the Plain that I soon decided a shorter
walk to the top of Chapman's Pool Hill would suffice. The skies threw
down rain which shifted into a horizontal plane, in terrible, blinding

gusts - the reality of the small and inoffensive word 'squall'. At Chapman's Pool Hill, where exposure to the wind suddenly increased, I was caught off-guard and thrown back against the stone wall with a jarring thud that knocked me sick. I beat a hasty retreat.

Captain Paynter's certificates arrived in the post one crisp February morning. The first thing that struck me was the captain's handwriting: ponderous and painstakingly formed letters, which reminded me of the style I had seen in Victorian lists of Methodist trustees, and the antithesis of Third Officer Donald's confident, flowing hand. It rather confirmed the impression I had of Captain Paynter as a man who had got where he had through hard work and dedication, rather than natural talent. The certificates revealed the many ships he had sailed in before joining the Hain company; nothing startling there. Then I turned to his application to be examined for his master's ticket at Plymouth dated 17 February 1904. My eye ran down to: '(D.) - If Candidate has failed in a previous Examination for the Certificate now required, he must here state when and where ...' The box beneath was filled in. He had been examined at Plymouth two days earlier: 'Subjects in which he failed ... Napiers Diagram.' I was so overcome by the surprise of finding a blemish on Captain Paynter's record and by sheer bewilderment, that I cursed at the top of my voice: 'What the hell is Napiers Diagram!'

I searched high and low, eventually finding an entry in the *Encyclopaedia of Nautical Knowledge* (Cornell Maritime Press). I read the entry. I went back and read the court's opinion on the cause of the stranding. I read the opinion again; then re-read the entry - back and forth I went:

The master of the *Treveal* in giving the compass course SE by E $1/2$ E to the third officer, stated there was half a point easterly deviation and the magnetic course would be SE by E ...

Had the deviation been half a point *West* instead of half a point *East* (as applied), the magnetic course would have been ESE. This course, if steered from the accepted point of departure would have passed close to the position given by the chief officer at Kimmeridge coastguard station for 8.40 p.m., viz - three miles west of the station, and almost exactly on to the spot where the *Treveal* struck the ground. Taking into consideration the last deviation of which records were produced was 3 W the Court considers it most probable that a deviation of the wrong name was applied and the course ESE (magnetic) made in consequence, which led the ship to danger.

Then the entry in the *Encyclopaedia of Nautical Knowledge*:

NAPIER'S DIAGRAM. A device in graphic form for facilitating conversion of magnetic courses to compass courses and vice versa from a deviation curve ... It consists of a vertical middle line graduated to represent degrees on rim of a compass-card from N. downward through E. Dotted lines sloping downward from left to right are drawn at a 60°angle with compass-rim line and plain lines at same angle upward from left to right, each of which lines cross at their intersection with the compass-rim line, usually at every 15°. Deviations from a set of observations are plotted on the appropriate *dotted lines*, where, as is usual, observations are those for ship's head *by compass*; if for *magnetic headings*, on the *plain lines*; scale used being that of the compass-rim and measured from latter along such line (or one parallel with it). Then a fair curve drawn through all plotted observed deviations indicates such values for any other courses on the compass-rim line. As illustrating use of the diagram in converting a *magnetic* course to a *compass* course, assume any heading on the compass-rim line; then follow *plain* line, or one parallel with it, from assumed heading toward the deviation curve and return to compass-rim line by following *dotted* line, or one parallel with it; point on compass-rim line is then *compass course* required. Since all sides of a 60° triangle are identical (equilateral), we thus simply have allowed deviation as indicated in the curve to the right or to the left, according to its name, with the assurance that it is applied *in the right direction*. Practical use of the diagram is nicely summed up in the old rhyme:
"*From compass course, magnetic course to gain,*
Depart by dotted and return by plain.
From magnetic course, to steer a course allotted,
Depart by plain and then return by dotted." (Original emphasis.)

Then back again to the opinion of the court on the cause of the stranding: 'the Court considers it most probable that *a deviation of the wrong name was applied*.' (My emphasis.)

I could hardly believe what I was reading. I didn't understand the details but it was clear that in Charles Paynter's failure to pass his first master's examination there was a precedent for the sort of error in navigation which took the *Treveal* on to the Kimmeridge Ledge.

As I set out to revisit St Ives in the early hours of an early summer morning, the road wide and empty as an ocean, my mind went over the whole disaster again.

On the night of 9 January 1920, Captain Paynter had made a navigational error in setting a course up Channel out of Weymouth Bay. Why he made the error at that particular time can never be known for certain. It had been a long voyage, the ship had come through bad weather and at Portland no pilot was waiting. Perhaps he was tired. Hain captains, with uncertificated or inexperienced officers aboard had to spend more time on the bridge than their counterparts in some other companies. Almost certainly Captain Paynter was tired. Perhaps his 'nerve' had simply been tested once too often. Whatever the reason, the mind of the captain, as the *Treveal* lay off Portland, was sufficiently weary, distracted or disturbed to succumb to an old weakness - the weakness which had been revealed when he sat his first examination for a master's certificate of competency.

Furthermore, his mind remained in the same state as the *Treveal* departed from Weymouth Bay, for he failed to see that he was headed out on the wrong course. Tired, distracted or disturbed (with perhaps a letter - among those brought out to the ship just before she departed - making further demands on his concentration), Captain Paynter, on a too cursory inspection of his surroundings, may have been deceived as to which way he was actually facing, as have other navigators been before him. Some have said that the world along Weymouth front seems to turn turtle. Dr Llewellyn Pridham, formerly of the Royal Navy, wrote, in *The Dorset Coastline* (p 44): 'There is one rather peculiar fact about Weymouth Bay. The visitor, knowing the town to be on the south coast, naturally enough thinks when he is standing on the sea front that he is facing south'ard. As a matter of fact he is looking east, even N.E. ...' Could Captain Paynter have fallen foul of this topographical peculiarity - looking at the world as if through a diver's helmet?

Certainly, at Weymouth Bay and in the hour before the *Treveal* struck the Kimmeridge Ledge Captain Paynter was 'not himself'. It can be seen, I think, in his reaction to Third Officer Donald reporting seeing the loom of land. The captain's first reaction was that Donald was mistaken. Donald himself had checked the course no fewer than six times, but his belief in what he had seen was strong enough for him to tell Captain Paynter a second time. What did the captain do? Tell the young upstart again that he was mistaken and in no uncertain terms? No. Accept what Donald had seen, thank his lucky starts for having such a sharp-eyed third officer and alter course boldly to the south? No. Captain Paynter was uncertain; lacking the confidence to take one firm line or the other. He ordered the course to be altered half a point to the south; half a point. It was not enough. He had, in the words of a local fisherman, 'got himself into a nasty corner.'

In such a corner his soul might be required of him - even before the dawn of the day. Perhaps God called quickly to Captain Paynter - as he called slowly to Edward Reed. Perhaps the great, grinding jolt - metal upon rock - sent him regressing back to the hard chapel pews of his early years. There, for sin, error, or human weakness of any kind, a terrible punishment lay in store. (It was perhaps Methodism which led Frank Lander to the belief that, 'If you do ninety-nine things right and the hundredth wrong, you'll always be remembered for the hundredth wrong.')

What of Captain Paynter's reaction as the tide drove his vessel further on to the Ledge? It is well known that commanders often 'go into denial' at the scene of a disaster for which they are responsible. Captain Kemp had shocked me at one stage of my interview with him, by suddenly blurting out, as I preceded a question with 'They didn't find the log book ': 'Oh no, that was immediately threw overboard I expect.' Whether that happened or not, Captain Paynter certainly appears not to have disclosed his navigational error to anybody else. Third Officer Donald and Chief Engineer Thirkell both later denied any knowledge of how the ship came to go ashore: it 'simply happened'. Yet it is almost impossible to believe that Captain Paynter, at some point during the long night of 9 / 10 January, didn't go back over the course he had set and discover the error he had made. Surely he did.

From compass course, magnetic course to gain,
Depart by dotted and return by plain.
From magnetic course, to steer a course allotted,
Depart by plain and then return by dotted.

Such a rhyme could insinuate itself into the mind of a man who had made the error the rhyme was intended to guard against. Yet if it did, or if he was otherwise haunted by his error, he showed (as far as can be gathered from the evidence) no external appearance of it. He was in command - even if his actions suggest a man who was denying the reality of the terrible danger that the ship and crew were in. He kept his navigation lights burning and his steam up. He called for tugs, salvage ships and lighters. Far into the night his one concern seemed to be to save his ship. What about his crew? Save our souls - 42 of them. Did he think their souls were safe enough? They hadn't made the error which might damn a man in the next life and in this destroy the years of hard work and dedication which enabled him to walk around the town of St Ives with his head held high.

Only in the morning, when the *Treveal* split her side, could Captain Paynter no longer deny the reality of the situation. As the day dawned and the mist swirled about did he perhaps feel: 'a presence - an imaginary shape or essence from the human multitude lying below; those who had gone down in vessels of war; East Indiamen, barges, brigs, and ships of the Armada - select people, common, and debased, whose interests and hopes had been as wide asunder as the poles, but who had rolled each other to oneness on that restless sea-bed ...' (Thomas Hardy: *The Well-Beloved*). Certainly Captain Paynter must have seen the fate of his crew if he didn't act quickly. The ship was doomed, he could no longer deny it, but the men could still be saved. Suddenly they were 'my people' and he was sending out the triple SOS wireless message and firing distress rockets. Into the lifeboats they went.

One can only imagine the depth of despair that Captain Paynter must have felt when the two boats capsized in Chapman's Pool.

At St Ives, I received the usual friendly welcome from Captain Kemp. I wanted his view on Captain Paynter's error and I got straight to the point.

Q. How do you think the captain could have made the mistake that led to the *Treveal* going on the Kimmeridge Ledge?

A. That's what everybody was asking. Portland must have frightened bloody Paynter somehow, I don't know why ...

Q. Its as if he had a brainstorm ... something really wrong somewhere. My grandfather used to say the fishermen had a saying - you know he was a lobster fisherman - and they had a saying that small boats keep in and large boats keep out, so he was on the lobster run, Charlie Paynter.

A. Yes, he was. I know sometimes the ships in them days, they went inside The Mole, and all inside when they should have kept outside. They were the captains that knew everything -

Q. I don't think that was Charlie Paynter, though: the inquiry thought he made an error, that he 'applied a deviation of the wrong name', so I suppose the question really is how did he not realise he had made an error with all the navigation aids, like the Shambles and the Portland light, around him?

A. Well, he might have come out of the chart room or his room and shouted up the course for them to steer, and he wasn't on the bridge, was he?

Q. He was.

A. Was he. Well, how the hell he didn't see he was so far off his course I don't know - Are you sure he was on the bridge?

Q. He was according to Donald.

(Captain Kemp shakes his head.)

Q. You don't think he was there?

A. He couldn't have been, could he? If he was keeping a visual look out he would have seen he was off his course.

Q. So where was Charlie Paynter if he wasn't on the bridge?

A. Well, I don't know. He might have done anything. He might have been taken short, but then on that the third officer who he left in charge - if Charlie Paynter was in any doubt at all, was to call the chief officer and make him go on the bridge. In a case like that I should have called the chief officer and said, 'Look, I'm taken short, or I'm taken sick. There's the course. Make sure you keep her off the reef.' So, there's a personal error by the captain whether he was on the bridge or he wasn't.

Q. And one with terrible consequences.

A. Terrible. I remember when the bodies were being brought back, the women down here were going through the streets saying 'My poor murdered boys' and blaming poor old Charlie for throwing their lives away. And I did hear that he didn't want to be picked up.

Q. How do you mean, didn't want to be picked up?

A. Well, when he's in the water somebody offered him his lifebelt and says 'Here, Captain Paynter, here's a help for you to get in' ...

Q. But he didn't accept it?

A. He didn't accept it. That's what I heard when I was at sea, because there were people from that ship, the *Treveal*, that transferred - Whether it was just a rumour, I don't know ... I suppose he was afraid of the consequences and I don't suppose he wanted to live, particularly in a town like this.

Emerging from Captain Kemp's house, the sunlight was almost blinding. My head reeled as much with what Captain Kemp had said as with the sun. The court that inquired into the loss of the *Treveal* had accepted

Third Officer Donald's evidence of what had occurred on the bridge before the ship went aground. Captain Kemp had suggested the possibility of a slightly different scenario: that Captain Paynter may not have been on the bridge. I weighed it up. It was speculation - the speculation of an experienced sea captain - but speculation all the same.

My final visit to the St Ives Museum produced another piece of information which opened the door of speculation further. In following up Third Officer Donald's post-*Treveal* career in the Hain company ledgers I was stunned to find the following entries:

Capacity	Steamer	Date of Appointment	Date of Leaving
3rd Mate	Tremorvah	16 June 1920	Aug 1921
2nd Mate	Trevanion	Feb 1922	24 Mar 1922
Dismissed for insobriety - see Uren's letter 24/3/22			
2nd Mate	Lena	15 May 1922	29 June 1923
See Uren's letter 16/8/22. Dismissed - see Uren's letter 2/9/23			

'Ah,' said Mr Stevens, at my shoulder.

'Does the museum by any chance have these letters of Uren's?' I asked.

The curator shook his head doubtfully.

'I think Uren must be Frederick Uren, who was Hains' marine superintendent at the time and involved in the *Treveal* inquiry,' I said.

'No,' said Mr Stevens. 'I've never come across any Uren's letters.'

I walked out of the museum for the last time and resolved, for my own part, to shut the door of speculation.

I walked around the St Ives harbour to the Tourist Information Office, where Captain Paynter's great niece, Mrs Beach, worked. I had followed up another lead on Captain Paynter, which had come to nothing, other than that the Paynter family tomb could be found in Barnoon Cemetery. I asked Mrs Beach if she would be kind enough to give me directions. She said she would accompany me. We walked up to the vast cemetery, Mrs Beach first pointing out in a quiet corner the Hain family tomb - the double headstone seemingly having been toppled, by wind or vandals, and half-heartedly and unprettily repaired with concrete and bitumen. Through row upon row of headstones we walked, every other one almost seeming to bear the inscription 'Master Mariner' or 'drowned' following one shipwreck or another.

'There it is,' said Mrs Beach suddenly.

My eye caught first a stone to Peter Cogar, the *Treveal*'s carpenter, 'WHO WAS DROWNED IN THE S.S. TREVEAL DISASTER'.

Next-door-but-one to the Cogar stone was the Paynter family grave. They were all there - mother and four children. The inscription to Captain Paynter read:

CHARLES PAYNTER

HER SON

WHO ENTERED INTO REST

JAN^Y 10TH 1920,

AGED 42 YEARS.

No mention of his status as Master Mariner. No mention of the manner of his death. These two omissions were surely a tacit acknowledgement by the family itself that Captain Charles Paynter's role in the *Treveal* disaster had not been one of distinction.

Mrs Beach hurried back to work, leaving me alone in the cemetery. I closed my eyes, suddenly overcome by weariness, and stood listening to the surf roaring on the beach below.

Epilogue

As I descend the steep, winding hill into Kimmeridge village, Clavell's Tower, formerly a coastguard look out, seems in the hands of an illusionist - now you see it, now you don't. Beyond the little village of stone walls and thatched roofs I turn right, along the road to the foreshore.

At Kimmeridge Bay the annual Sea Sunday Service is about to commence. I seat myself amongst those already gathered. Our pews are bales of straw, arranged in a crescent. The vicar, of good voice and mien, welcomes us and leads us into the opening hymn, 'Eternal Father strong to save.' Around me, voices of diverse tone and timbre swell into one voice, which is carried away on the breeze to wander among the high keening shrills of seagulls.

I blink in the glare of the bright sun. To the west a broad sweep of hills is divided into fields, and the cottages at Goulter look dull grey, with ten chimneys, each casting the same angle of shadow. To the south is the Kimmeridge Ledge. The wreck of the *Treveal* lies silent and rusting, its exact location known only to divers and fishermen. Today there are few souvenirs left for divers, and fishermen say that shellfish hauled from the spot are no longer stained blood red. The sea ebbs and flows. When I joined the Merchant Navy in 1954 and stepped aboard a ship bound for New Zealand I thought how large the vessel looked at her berth. Yet soon I realised she displaced but a drop in the ocean. One day the great power of the sea will wash the Kimmeridge Ledge clean of the last remnant of the *Treveal*. On that day, perhaps, as the tide turns, the ghosts of Captain Paynter and the crew will walk out ashore, before thinning away forever.

The vicar concludes the service with the blessing: 'We commend to your keeping all those who sail the seas.' Dusk falls lightly on Kimmeridge Bay, and with it the last breeze from the sun. The makeshift altar, a trestle table covered with a white sheet, is about to be packed away, along with a small cross-fashioned from a bronze fitting salvaged from the *Treveal*.

For me, at any rate, the long quest has ended.